Synchronicity as the Work of the Holy Spirit

Synchronicity as the Work
of the Holy Spirit

Synchronicity as the Work of the Holy Spirit

Jungian Insights for Spiritual Direction and Pastoral Ministry

Lex Ferrauiola

Tenafly, New Jersey

Summer 2011

Copyright © 2011 by Lex Ferrauiola
All rights reserved.

For Wanda, my sweetheart and best friend.

You are the sun and the moon and the stars.

Table of Contents

Preface   11

Chapter One: Introduction   13

     The Work of the Holy Spirit   13

     The Unconscious as Workplace of the Holy Spirit   15

         Jungian Insights into the Unconscious   16

         Synchronicity as a Message from the Unconscious   18

     The Place of Synchronicity within Pastoral Ministry   20

     Structure and Value of this Research   23

     Synchronicity as the Work of the Holy Spirit   25

Chapter Two: Literature Review   27

     The Work of the Holy Spirit as Seen in Christian Theology   27

     The Phenomenon of Synchronicity   33

         Twentieth Century Jungian Insights   33

             Individuation: the Drive to Wholeness   34

             The Collective Unconscious: the God Within   35

         Synchronicity   38

         Illuminating the Promptings of the Holy Spirit   41

Table of Contents (cont'd)

Chapter Three: Synchronicity Analyzed   44

    Guiding the Individual to Wholeness   45

        In the Psyche   45

        In the Soul   46

    Similarities between Individuation and Sanctification   49

    The Holy Spirit as Ringmaster of Sanctification   50

    Synchronicity at Work in the Lives of Saints and Mystics   52

        Saint Francis of Assisi   54

    Synchronicity at Work in Ordinary Time   55

        Baby Kathleen   56

        The Brothers Fletcher   57

        A Friend Named Fox   57

    Individuation and Sanctification: The Role of Freedom   59

Chapter Four: Synchronicity in the Practice of Spiritual Direction   62

    Ministry of Spiritual Direction   63

    Use of Metaphor in Spiritual Direction   64

    Role of Spiritual Director in Jungian-based Direction   65

Table of Contents (cont'd)

Jungian Insights Applied to Spiritual Direction   67

    The Unconscious   67

    Individuation and Conversion   68

    Obstacles to the Work of the Holy Spirit   69

    Synchronicity in Spiritual Direction   72

Synchronicity and Its Impact   73

Chapter Five: Reflection and Analysis   74

    Insights from this Project   74

    Implications of Research   75

        For the IPM   75

        For Ecclesial Teaching and Pastoral Practice   76

        For Ministry   77

Chapter Six: Future Directions   78

    Contributions of this Research to Pastoral Ministry   78

    Pastoral Areas for Further Research   79

    On to the Future   81

Table of Contents (cont'd)

Appendix: A Personal Experience of Synchronicity and Its Impact   83

Works Cited   89

Preface

The Second Vatican Council in the 1960s reawakened the consciousness of the Church to the active presence of the Holy Spirit in the world. The Council reminded us that it is through God's Spirit that we are led to truth and, ultimately, to salvation. Since the Council, the Church has urged us to be attentive and responsive to the promptings of the Holy Spirit in our lives – while at the same time cautioning us that those promptings can be difficult to discern.

Over the last ten years I have been very much drawn to the Holy Spirit. As part of graduate studies in Pastoral Ministry at Saint Mary's University of Minnesota, I researched ways in which the Holy Spirit makes itself known to us. My master's thesis held that one way in which the Holy Spirit prompts us is through our experience of synchronicity. This book represents that thesis.

The word 'synchronicity' is a term used by the psychologist Carl Jung to describe the experience of meaningful coincidences that are not causally related; coincidences that are not merely accidents or good fortune, but, as Jung believed, signs created by an integrated and purposeful universe to touch the lives of individuals and lead them to integration and wholeness; coincidences that we experience as if God were winking at us, pulling our sleeve, trying to get our attention, and pointing the way. I have had these experiences, and whenever I speak about them people are quick to share their own. Our experiences of synchronicity are the promptings of the Holy Spirit at work within our lives.

As Christians we believe in a God who loves each human being as if he or she were the only person in the world; a God who is not content to stand by patiently in the wings, hoping and waiting for us to come home, but who passionately pursues us through life – like a 'hound of heaven' – lest we lose our way.

The Holy Spirit is always pursuing us with signs that call us to pay attention. If we recognize and act upon these signs, they can lead us to wholeness and holiness. Synchronistic events that occur throughout our life create a 'highway' on which the Holy Spirit travels to reach and guide us – but we must be attentive and responsive to these promptings.

But that's not always so easy. Being attentive requires that we be truly present: present to God, present to others, and present to self. God can only be found in the present; not in what might have been, or what might be, but in what *is*. It is in the present, the now, that the Holy Spirit is always by our side, trying to get our attention, trying to show us the way.

The twentieth century Jungian insight into synchronicity can provide us twenty-first century spiritual directors with a new language and understanding for discerning and illuminating the presence and promptings of the Holy Spirit at work in the lives of those to whom we minister.

Synchronicity is the work of the Holy Spirit tapping us on the shoulder and pointing the way to healing, wholeness and sanctification.

We just have to be listening.

*

This book is a revised version of an IPR (Integrated Pastoral Research thesis) submitted by the author in completion of a Master of Arts graduate degree (2007) in Pastoral Ministry at the Institute for Pastoral Ministry (IPM) within Saint Mary's University of Minnesota. I would like to acknowledge and thank two special people who helped and supported me in the writing of my thesis, and without whose help this book would not have been written: my spiritual director Brother Donald Bisson, FMS; and my graduate thesis advisor at Saint Mary's Dr. Susan Windley Daoust.

Lex Ferrauiola
Tenafly, New Jersey
deaconlex@gmail.com

Chapter One: Introduction

Carl Gustav Jung (1875–1961), father of analytical psychology, explored the unconscious and gave the world insights and a language of metaphors to discern and communicate its processes and constructs, and to guide the individual on the path to psychological and spiritual integration. The phenomenon of synchronicity is one of Jung's major insights. Synchronicity is the experience of meaningful coincidences that are not causally related; coincidences that are not merely accidents or good fortune, but signs created by an integrated and purposeful universe to touch the lives of individuals and lead them to integration and wholeness. It is the thesis of this research project that the experience of synchronicity is the work of the Holy Spirit guiding each soul to healing, wholeness and sanctification; and that this twentieth century Jungian insight can provide psychologically attuned twenty-first century pastoral ministers with a new language and understanding to discern and illuminate the presence and promptings of the Holy Spirit at work in the lives of those to whom they minister.

The Work of the Holy Spirit

It is through God's Spirit that human beings are sanctified. As Catholics we believe in an immanent and personal God: one who is not content to stand in the wings, hoping and waiting for us to come home, but who passionately pursues us through life like a 'hound of heaven' lest we lose our way. Throughout this pursuit God's Spirit is always speaking to us with signs that call us to pay attention. If we recognize and act upon these signs, they can lead us to wholeness and holiness.

Throughout the first fifteen hundred years of Christianity, the Holy Spirit was looked to as the soul's guiding light. Saint Augustine recognized and preached that the Holy Spirit operates in the deepest level of the human soul as the "longing that impels us toward God and causes us to end in him" (Congar Vol. I, 81). Saint Symeon, Greek Christian mystic of the eleventh century, taught those who came to him for spiritual direction that the way to wholeness is through "the illumination of the Spirit" (Jaoudi 44). Medieval saints experienced and wrote about the Holy Spirit as present in their hearts and working in their lives. Saint Catherine of Sienna asks her readers who are suffering "to trust that the Spirit will inspire someone to bring needed aid" (Dreyer 149). The writings and preaching of Christian mystics reveal deeply personal experiences of the Holy Spirit's presence inwardly in self-encounter, and intuitively beneath the level of consciousness.

With the Enlightenment and the onset of modern times, Pneumatology was overshadowed by Christology; personal awareness of and relationship with the Holy Spirit faded from the theological stage. Modern believers in the West were intellectually more comfortable relating to the historical Christ, whom they could outwardly visualize and hear through the Gospels, than to the Holy Spirit, who required inward intuitive experience and self-encounter. Though always venerated as an equal member in good standing of the Blessed Trinity, the Holy Spirit was not perceived as a prime mover in the soul's journey toward wholeness. The Spirit fell into the background and became what Jürgen Moltmann has referred to as "the Cinderella of Western theology" (*The Spirit* 1).

Increasing attention has been given to the Holy Spirit since the middle of the twentieth century. In *Advents of the Spirit*, a collection of essays on the reemergence of Pneumatology, Hinze and Dabney argue that the failure of technology is a factor in the renewed interest and respect being given to the Holy Spirit. Western society's dream of technology as the panacea for humanity has proven to also be its bane. Technology that has produced medicine and manufacturing has also led to poisoned water and air and to weapons of mass destruction as well (21).

Another factor in this renewed interest is presented by Philip Clayton in *Advents of the Spirit*. He attributes this new freedom to speak about the Holy Spirit to a shift in theological perspective from substance to spirit ontology: an evolution in theology from medieval metaphysical structures where every person as well as God was viewed as a separate substance, subject to the principles of hierarchy, goal-directedness and order, to a new perspective where spirit is no longer boxed into the category of substance, but exists as an ontological principle in its own right (181). Clayton makes the case that once the spiritual side of personhood became emergent, there occurred a renewed interest in a higher spiritual being that transcends the world; for Christians the Holy Spirit was reintroduced as a higher ontological culminating level, "above the level of embodied spirit that characterizes human experience" (191).

In the mid 1960s the Fathers of the Second Vatican Council reminded the faithful that the Holy Spirit actively operates in the lives of individuals, calling them to wholeness and leading them to sanctification. The *Dogmatic Constitution on Divine Revelation* reawakened the consciousness of the Church to the active presence of the Holy Spirit in the life of each human being, and reminded believers that it is through God's Spirit that Christians are led to truth (Vatican II 102).

This new advent of the Spirit has led modern Christian theologians, among them Congar, McDonnell, Kilmartin and Moltmann, to write and preach extensively on the activity of the Holy Spirit in the world. They have used metaphors to describe the Holy Spirit: as a God of surprises who is known to us not directly as a unique personality, but through the movement and spiritual growth he brings about within us; as the place of mediation, whereby God touches the individual and sets him or her on the road back to God; as "the unrestricted presence of God in which our life wakes up" (Moltmann, *The Source* 11); as a God who is continuously tapping us on the shoulder and pulling our coat, forever calling us home. Since this new advent of the Spirit, the Church has urged believers to be attentive and receptive to the promptings of the Holy Spirit, while noting that the Spirit's presence and activity, its cues and messages, are often difficult to discern within the limits of the conscious mind.

The Unconscious as Workplace of the Holy Spirit

Parallel with this reawakening by the Church to the presence and promptings of the Holy Spirit, knowledge of the unconscious mind was slowly emerging along with the associated science of depth psychology. Educated and influenced by psychology, theologians and pastoral ministers began to understand that in its unbounded and undeterred love for each person, the Holy Spirit often speaks to the individual through the unconscious. Jesuit Father George J. Schemel has written that the evolution of depth psychology that occurred in the twentieth century has led pastoral ministers, especially those involved in spiritual direction, to take into account the "place of the unconscious in spiritual direction and in people's lives" (1). Schemel went further to argue that while the traditional practice of spiritual direction focuses on the director's dialogue with the directee's conscious ego, fulfilling Jesus' command to love God with one's whole soul requires the individual to give God not only the ego but one's whole self, "conscious as well as unconscious" (6).

Sigmund Freud and Carl Gustav Jung were pioneers and prophets in the science of depth psychology. Where Freud's theory of psychoanalysis was based on causation in matter, Jung's analytical psychology was teleological: the goal being psychological and spiritual wholeness. Freud reduced every psychological process to material causation with its genesis in "sexual trauma and shock" (Bair 86). Jung, on the other hand, understood instinctual drives, including sexuality, as "symbols of spiritual forces conducive to health" (86). Father Victor White, Dominican theologian and friend of Jung's, wrote that "whereas for Freud religion is a symptom of psychological disease, for Jung the absence of religion is at the root of all adult psychological disease" (47). Where Freud dismissed religion as an illusion, Jung saw it as the means to psychological health. For Jung, the path to wholeness was through the unconscious.

Jungian Insights into the Unconscious

Through his years of practice as a psychiatrist and decades of studying religion, spirituality, myth and culture, Jung explored the unconscious and gave the world insights and a language of metaphors to describe and communicate its processes and constructs. These tools can be used to guide the individual on the path to psychological and spiritual wholeness. Among Jung's wide spectrum of thought, he is perhaps best known for his theories on individuation, the collective unconscious, and the phenomenon of synchronicity. While the focus of this research is synchronicity as the work of the Holy Spirit, an understanding of synchronicity and how it relates to the soul's journey to sanctification requires an understanding of individuation and the collective unconscious.

Just as the human body is designed to grow into its fullest physical potential, the human psyche is designed to integrate into a balanced whole, a Self. The psyche is innately driven to differentiate into selfhood through a process Jung named individuation. Through individuation all forces within the psyche become conscious, balanced and fully developed to bring it to its inherent wholeness. Individuation is a process of lifelong struggle and growth; a personal journey towards acceptance of and wholeness with a transcendent function, the Self, operating within the unconscious psyche of every human being.

Driven by the need for psychological and spiritual wholeness, the individual consciously grows to recognize and be at one with his or her true, unique and complete Self. Jung viewed the psyche as an integrated whole, not as the sum of its parts. The state of wholeness in the psyche may be thought of as a secular analogy to what Christians define as holiness in the soul. This IPR maintains that what Jung describes in psychological terms as individuation is a stage on the journey towards what Catholic theologians refer to as sanctification: a spiritual process that goes on within the human psyche, whereby the Holy Spirit brings the innate desire for God into consciousness and works within the soul to guide the individual to recognize and willingly embrace God for eternity.

For Jung there is a dimension within each person that reflects both the depths of the individual's human psyche, or soul and the depths of all creation — past, present and future. Jung named this dimension the collective unconscious. It contains unconscious reflections of the larger universe: reflections within the microcosm of the individual that take the form of archetypes, the term Jung used for images that symbolically represent universal aspects of the macrocosm. In *Memories, Dreams and Re-*

flections, the memoir he dictated as he neared the end of his life, Jung stated that the human psyche is set up in accord with the structure of the universe, and that whatever happens "in the macrocosm likewise happens in the infinitesimal and most subjective reaches of the psyche." Jung added that where he prefers the term 'the unconscious,' he might "equally well speak of God" (335–340).

In Jung's early writing, wholeness, i.e., the integrated Self, was described as being fully contained within the deepest levels of the human psyche. The Self was ensconced within the collective unconscious, this repository of innate memories and emotive images — archetypes genetically transmitted and enhanced through millions of years of human evolution. Before his death, Jung understood that the human psyche responds not only to intrapsychic forces pulling it toward individual psychological wholeness, but to a transcendental force drawing all things toward a universal spiritual wholeness. It is through the collective unconscious that the individual becomes not only whole, but also coextensive with the totality of the cosmos.

Jung maintained that there exists, "in the deepest levels of the psyche," the presence of a transcendental force, an "absolute knowledge" that moves into consciousness and provides the individual with "insights into the events of outer reality, past, present, and future" (Aziz 111). The Trinitarian theology of Edward Kilmartin holds that human beings are created with an "orientation towards the Transcendent" and that it is through the Holy Spirit that human beings are led to the fulfillment of that orientation in "personal union with God" (Hall 134). This research maintains that what Jung referred to in psychological terms as an absolute knowledge within the collective unconscious describes the indwelling presence of the Holy Spirit, prompting conscious recognition and urging the individual soul to wholeness, sanctification and union with its creator.

Synchronicity as a Message from the Unconscious

Jung argued that there are signposts along the road to individuation: messages from the unconscious. These messages are brought to conscious awareness by psychic energy activated by archetypal images, by the interpretation of dreams and active imagination, and by the recognition of synchronistic events and patterns in one's environment. He maintained that the unconscious intervened in the individuation journey, and that when this intervention occurs, an acausal relationship between the psyche and surrounding physical events presents itself to conscious awareness. This awareness is the phenomenon of synchronicity: a meaningful coincidence in which external events or dreams "symbolize what is happening in the psyche" (McMichaels 98). It is the bridge between the unconscious and physical events. In the synchronistic event there is a coming together of what appears to be chance factors, not causally linked, that prove themselves to be meaningfully related and "at the very heart of the process by which the purpose of the individual's life unfolds and becomes his fate" (Progoff, *Jung* 64).

In his essay "A Psychological Approach to the Trinity," Jung interprets the theological statement that dogmas are inspired by the Holy Spirit as indicating that they are "not the product of conscious cogitation and speculation, but are motivated from sources outside consciousness and possibly even outside man" (150). The major role in the individuation process was in fact given to the Holy Spirit, whom Jung identified as the "very principle of psychic wholeness and the bridge between human experience and the Godhead" (Lammers 162). To cross that bridge the human being must become conscious of wholeness, not merely within the psyche but present within the universe and seen through the synchronistic patterning of events in one's environment.

Jung called that powerful force revealing itself and calling individuals to wholeness through synchronicity the Holy Spirit. However, Jung was never sure if this principle of psychic wholeness, this Holy Spirit, was a self-contained energy within the individual's collective unconscious, or, in fact, a transcendent conscious energy that beckoned, and existed independent of, the individual. Herein lays the great divide between Jungian depth psychology and Christian theology. Jung was agnostic about the source and essence of the Holy Spirit: it might be purely interpsychic energy, hard-wired in the individual's unconscious to draw one to psychological and spiritual wholeness; or it might be an external and impersonal cosmic force gathering all living things into quantum harmony. For the Christian there is no ambiguity — the Holy Spirit is the other hand of God, beckoning the soul home.

Squire Rushnell refers to synchronistic events as 'God Winks,' "little messages" to the soul on the journey through life, nudging the individual along the grand path that has been designed for him or her by God (xiii). Writing on Jung's concept of synchronicity in *The Road Less Traveled*, M. Scott Peck held that the commonality of synchronistic experiences is an indication that "these phenomena are part of or manifestations of a single phenomenon: a powerful force originating outside of human consciousness which nurtures the spiritual growth of human beings" (260). This research holds that that powerful force, revealing itself and calling individuals to wholeness, is the Holy Spirit; and that synchronicity is the work of God's Spirit to get one's attention and point the way.

The Place of Synchronicity within Pastoral Ministry

Catholic tradition teaches that prayer, communal liturgy, scripture and spiritual reading serve as "major sources" of spiritual development (McBrien 1214). Marist Brother Donald Bisson, pioneer in the use of analytical psychology for the ministry of spiritual direction, holds that "God speaks within the realms of sacraments, prayer, scripture and history and in the human soul" as well (39). The pastoral minister is called "to listen with a discerning heart and mind to the pull of God from the depths [of the soul] as well as from the community of faith" (219). Jungian insights and metaphors can be used in ministry to express the language of the soul. The twentieth century Jungian insight of synchronicity can help the contemporary Catholic pastoral minister, enlightened and influenced by knowledge of the unconscious and psychology, to discern and illuminate the cues and pushes of the Holy Spirit on the individual's journey to wholeness and sanctification.

A distinction between the Jungian analyst and the pastoral minister must be clearly understood: where the Jungian analyst understands the transcendent function of wholeness to reside and be attainable within the individual, the pastoral minister understands it to be integrated both within and without, and enabled by the presence and guidance of the Holy Spirit. The use of Jungian insights in pastoral ministry to discern the promptings of the Holy Spirit can lead the soul through stages of individuation and spiritual development to recognize and embrace its authentic Self. But, unlike it is in Jungian analysis, that internal embrace is not the end of the process. The grace of the Holy Spirit not only enables but pushes that inner Self outward, beyond individuation and through stages of conversion. This allows the inner Self to recognize the universal Self that transcends all creation, God; and to let go of the ego and allow the unconditional love of God to embrace, envelop and overwhelm the soul.

For Jung, the experience of synchronicity can lead to individuation; but individuation goes only part way towards what Christian theologians refer to as sanctification. The ideal of individuation is a wholly integrated Self within the psyche. Sanctification goes far beyond individuation: it is a spiritual process whereby the Holy Spirit awakens the innate longing for God within one's conscious mind and draws the soul to God. For that process to occur, desire for and identification with God as the external, transcendent, personal and loving creator must move out of its initial unconscious state and into consciousness, where it can be recognized, embraced, and acted upon by the will. In short, one turns outward and embraces and allows oneself to be embraced by God, the source of all goodness and love.

The Holy Spirit uses the experience of synchronicity to tap one on the shoulder and call the self-centered and defensive ego outward, to God. Where ego transcendence is the end goal of Jungian individuation, it is only a step on the journey to sanctification. For Christians, the Holy Spirit is the ringmaster of synchronicity and sanctification, and pastoral ministry is often the arena. An informed ministry that uses Jungian insights to discern and communicate the promptings of the Holy Spirit calls the individual soul to transcend ego and embrace its authentic

Self. Through the love that exists in that space of self-transcendence, one's true Self embraces the Self of God and experiences the beginnings of wholeness. It is the Holy Spirit who works in this space, and "makes possible and furthers our relation to God" (Hilberath 288).

On the journey to individuation and sanctification, the individual faces moments of crisis and conversion. It is in those moments, those desert experiences when ego defenses come down, that the Holy Spirit can reach and guide, cue and push one to wholeness. Using Jungian insights into the workings of the unconscious and the phenomenon of synchronicity, the trained pastoral minister can help the individual interpret those cues and pushes and recognize his or her authentic Self, and ultimately be embraced by God, the source of all wholeness. Bisson describes this recognition as "discernment of freedom for the availability of God" (219).

The pastoral minister trained in Jungian insights can guide those with whom he or she ministers to interpret synchronistic events as the work of the Holy Spirit — the cues and messages, pushes and pulls that illuminate the way to spiritual wholeness and sanctification. For both the Jungian analyst and the Catholic pastoral minister, the awareness of meaningful coincidence is the phenomenon of synchronicity. However, for the analyst synchronicity is perceived as connecting the unconscious and physical events; whereas for the pastoral minister it is the seen through the eyes of faith as being the other hand of God pointing the way.

In Jungian theory the energy released through archetypal activation generates synchronistic events that "connect the physical and psychic realms and provide a profound sense of meaningfulness through the overlap of two seemingly disconnected levels of reality" (McMichaels 105). In Christian theology it is God who intervenes in the physical world interacting with the natural order to present the soul with this sense of meaningfulness.

Victor White, Catholic priest and Jungian analyst, held that synchronistic experiences emanate from the Holy Spirit, which is God's presence residing within and calling each soul to wholeness. Synchronistic events that occur throughout one's life create a 'highway' on which the Holy Spirit travels to reach and guide us.

On the soul's faith journey, Jungian insights and metaphors can be used, particularly in the pastoral ministry of spiritual direction, as tools to express the inner language of the soul. These twentieth century Jungian insights can help the twenty-first century Christian, enlightened and influenced with knowledge of the unconscious, to discern the cues and pushes of the Holy Spirit on the journey to wholeness and sanctification. Through prayer and training in Jungian insights, the spiritual director can guide those in her or his care through the journey of the soul. These insights and tools empower one to minister to the "whole person in the spiritual journey from the outer and inner perspectives" (Bisson 82).

By enabling communication and integration between the conscious and the unconscious, and thereby illuminating synchronistic events, Jungian insights and language in pastoral ministry can aid the Holy Spirit to push and pull the individual toward healing and wholeness. For that wholeness to be complete, it must extend beyond the individual to be integrated with God. The recognition of synchronicity in Jungian analysis can lead the ego to integrate its projections and transcend itself, thereby enabling the individual to embrace his or her authentic Self. Pastoral ministry does not stop with the individuated, integrated Self; it seeks to help the soul to recognize the activity of the Holy Spirit as that Spirit leads the individual Self towards integration with the universal Self, God. A pastoral ministry that uses Jungian insights and metaphors to illuminate God's hand in everyday life can lead the soul to recognize and become its authentic Self; in so doing, one is free to recognize and become enveloped by and with the unconditional love of God, the universal Self of all creation.

Structure and Value of this Research

The purpose of this research was to analyze the Jungian concept of synchronicity in relation to the theology of the Holy Spirit and the Spirit's active role in guiding each human soul to sanctification. From the onset, the thesis of this research has been that the experience of synchronicity is the work of the Holy Spirit guiding each soul to healing, wholeness and sanctification; and that this twentieth century Jungian insight can provide psychologically attuned twenty-first century pastoral ministers with a new language and understanding for discerning and illuminating the presence and promptings of the Holy Spirit at work in the lives of those to whom they minister. The research presented in detail in the following chapters supports this thesis.

While reviewing the theology of the Holy Spirit, the writings of Jung, the Catholic tradition of spirituality, and the writings of contemporaries relating experiences of synchronicity, parallels were found in the language and metaphors used to describe human spiritual development and the activity of the Holy Spirit. These parallels are described in the review of academic literature in Chapter Two.

Chapter Three contains a broad analysis of this research thesis. Using a qualitative approach it explores and interprets how synchronicity presents itself as the individual passes through stages to individuation, or psychological wholeness, and is guided by the Holy Spirit beyond individuation to a state of spiritual wholeness, or sanctification. Examples of synchronicity throughout the ages are discussed in the form of selected experiences of saints and ordinary people — experiences which might be considered examples of synchronicity.

Chapter Four examines a specific application of this research thesis within the pastoral ministry of spiritual direction. An established practice of spiritual direction, one that uses the Jungian insight of synchronicity to discern the prompting of the Holy Spirit, is presented.

Chapter Five contains a reflection and analysis of insights and conclusions drawn from this project. It discusses the implications of this research for the IPM, general ecclesial teaching and ministry.

Chapter Six considers the value of this research to the field of pastoral ministry and the possibilities for future research and implementations. As argued in this final chapter, the use of the Jungian insight of synchronicity to illuminate the traditional

Catholic understanding of the Holy Spirit's activity in the lives of individuals may be further researched and creatively applied in many areas of pastoral ministry. The pastoral minister, trained with Jungian insights to recognize synchronistic experiences, can guide those with whom he or she ministers to interpret liturgical, sacramental and meditative experiences, as well as to positively address preparatory, transitional and degenerative life experiences. The pastoral minister with an understanding of Jungian insights can listen, interpret synchronistic experiences and dreams, and pose meaningful questions that not only discern and communicate the promptings of the Holy Spirit, but also encourage recognition and withdrawal of psychological projections. Once these projections are withdrawn, the individual is freer to recognize, accept and embrace her or his authentic Self, as well as the authenticity of others.

The Appendix contains a personal reflection that describes a powerful transformative experience of synchronicity: an experience that occurred during research for this project after I began spiritual direction with Brother Donald Bisson.

Through the many expressions of pastoral ministry, including spiritual direction, catechesis, liturgy, preaching, teaching, and small group sharing, ministers of the Church can use the Jungian language of synchronicity to illuminate and raise the threshold of receptivity to the Holy Spirit's promptings in the lives of others. By so doing, these pastoral ministers may themselves become, in effect, instruments of the Holy Spirit and collaborators in the soul's journey to sanctification.

Synchronicity as the Work of the Holy Spirit

John Pratt, in an article on synchronicity for Meridian Magazine, poses two interesting questions: was it merely coincidence that Ishmaelite traders happened by in time to save Joseph's life and transport him to Egypt (*Jerusalem Bible*, Gen. 37.28)? Or that Pharaoh's daughter went down that day to bathe in the river (Exod. 2.5-6)? Had these events never happened, the house of Israel and the Messiah might not have become reality.

And what if Joseph's dream had not reassured him to marry Mary (Matt. 1.20)? What if the Magi's dream hadn't led them to evade Herod's evil plan (Matt. 2.12)? Are those roses that mysteriously appear after one prays to Saint Therese mere coincidence? Was the vision of Constantine that led him to protect his soldiers with the sign of the cross and to establish the institutional Church just a hallucination? Whose voice spoke to Saint Francis from the cross in San Damiano telling him to rebuild the Church, and where did it come from?

On Sunday June 20, 2004 I was in the back seat of a taxi traveling to Saint Mary's University in Winona, Minnesota for the first time. Doubts arose as to the value, at age 57, of pursuing graduate work in pastoral ministry, spending two weeks away from family, and giving up vacation. I was considering withdrawing from class and catching the next flight back to New Jersey. A car, heading in the same direction, sped by with 'LEX' as the prefix on the license plate. The doubts continued. Five minutes went by and another car sped by; 'LEX' again but on a different plate. The doubts went away, the taxi arrived at Saint Mary's, and the journey continues. The meaningfulness of this 'God Wink' became the inspiration for this IPR project.

Chapter Two: Literature Review

This review of foundational literature focused on two questions: what is the work of the Holy Spirit as seen in Christian theology, and how might the phenomenon that Jung named synchronicity be seen as the work of the Holy Spirit? As such, this literature review was the starting point for validating the argument that the experience of synchronicity is the work of the Holy Spirit guiding each soul to healing, wholeness and sanctification; and that this twentieth century Jungian insight can provide psychologically attuned twenty-first century pastoral ministers with a new language and understanding for illuminating and discerning the presence and promptings of the Holy Spirit at work in their own lives and the lives of others.

The Work of the Holy Spirit as Seen in Christian Theology

Throughout the unfolding of the Judeo Christian tradition, theologians have used imagery and analogy to describe the active presence and the work of God's Spirit in the world. George Montague traces the development of imagery for the Holy Spirit in Scripture from life-breath, to wind, to fire, to water, to cloud, to dove, and finally to Paraclete. As this imagery evolved from the material world, through the animal world, and into the personal world, each image contributed to a growing understanding of "the mystery of the Spirit" and the conviction that God is its source (*Advents* 35, 60). Referencing Romans, Kilian McDonnell interprets Paul's understanding of the Spirit as "God's outgoing activity and presence to the world in a creative, quickening, renewing way" (6). Yves Congar follows the trace through the Patristics where the Spirit was believed to be secretly guiding God's work in the world. He writes that for Irenaeus, the Holy Spirit was like a theatrical producer, a George Lucas or Mel Brooks so to speak, "directing the drama of salvation on the stage of history" in such an intimate and personal way that individuals "know" the Spirit and "allow themselves to be seized" by it and become players in its work in the world (Vol. II, 220).

Medieval mystics experienced the Holy Spirit as alive and working in their lives. Saint Symeon, whom Congar names as one of the greatest Christian mystics, communicated a new type of personal experience of God: " 'You did not leave me lying, defiling myself in the mud . . . you sent for me and made me rise up out of this swamp' " (Vol. I, 93). For Saint Catherine of Sienna, the Holy Spirit was "not on the sidelines in God's relationship with the human community" (Dreyer 149), but actively present. Interpreting Catherine's experience of the Holy Spirit, Elizabeth Dreyer writes that "God's providence is reliable because the Holy Spirit is alive and well and acting throughout salvation history" (149). Catherine believed, and asks her readers who are in distress to trust, that "the Spirit will inspire someone to bring them aid" (149).

As the Western mind moved away from the heart and into the head, the Holy Spirit became what Jürgen Moltmann called "the Cinderella of Western theology" (*The Spirit* 1). Pneumatology was overshadowed by Christology; perhaps because the Church and the faithful were more comfortable relating consciously to the historical Christ, whom they could encounter through the Gospel, than to the Spirit, whom they could only feel. Rather than an outward experience of the Holy Spirit in the community, mystics experienced its presence, to a much greater degree, "inwardly, in self-encounter . . . [in] the simple words: 'God loves me' " (3). For Moltmann, the Spirit dwells in our hearts beneath our conscious level; it "rouses all our senses, permeates the unconscious too, and quickens the body, giving it a new life" (3).

In the introduction to *Advents of the Spirit,* a collection of essays on the current study of Pneumatology, Bradford Hinze and D. Lyle Dabney write that "increasing attention has been given to the Spirit and to Pneumatology during the second half of the twentieth century" (17). They identify one significant factor contributing to this increased attention and the reemergence of the doctrine of the Holy Spirit: the failure of technology. Rather than turning out to be a boon or panacea, Western society's dream of a technological society has proven to also be its bane: "the very science that has produced modern medicine, agriculture, manufacturing, travel, and communication is also that which poisons our water and air . . . and holds us hostage to weapons of mass destruction" (21). They speak of a chorus of new voices, "from psychologists, biologists, physicists, and philosophers to pop commentators and gurus" who have turned in hope to "the language of 'spirit' as that which speaks of something more and something other"; something other than us and what we know, something that can bring us salvation (21).

Philip Clayton, in his essay in the same book, attributes this new freedom to speak of the Holy Spirit to the removal of a particular metaphysical structure, what he refers to as "substance ontology" (176), where every person as well as God was viewed as a separate substance. Clayton believes that the most important single change in modern thought was the "movement from substance to spirit" (181); a movement "where *spirit* came to be defined not as a special case of a more general category, substance, but as a foundational ontological principle in its own right" (181). This marked a major "transformation from the medieval period, where the Spirit represented an objective metaphysical principle, tied closely with principles such as order, appropriate place in the hierarchy of being, goal-directedness or universal teleology, and the ontological separation between God and the world" (181).

Clayton argues that the human spirit is an "emergent phenomenon insofar as it is not reducible to the physical . . ." (191). This new hope in the human spirit stands in opposition to the "reductionist theories of the person," held by science and government, where the human person is explained in terms of "underlying neural structures, or biochemistry, or even quantum-physical events" (191). Clayton argues that once the spiritual side of personhood emerged there was a renewed interest among theists in a higher spiritual being "that transcends the world. . . " (191). For Christians, the Holy Spirit was reintroduced as a "higher . . . ontological . . . culminating level — above the level of embodied spirit that characterizes human experience" (191).

Clayton makes the connection between the spirit of the individual that transcends his or her physical structure, and the Spirit of the cosmos. "Just as *spirit* is the dimension of personal being that we only find in conjunction with highly complex physcal systems such as the human body, so God can be introduced as that spiritual identity, presence, and agency that we come to know out of the physical world (the universe) taken as a whole" (192). He argues that the reemergence of Pneumatology involves a "two-fold transformation of our own experience of spirit . . . " (194): we first "extrapolate from the qualities of spirit known [to us directly] through the natural world and through encounters with other human persons, augmenting them to the level appropriate to divine Spirit . . . "; and then we analogize the nature of the God-Spirit "based on our experience as embodied agents" (194).

With this reemergence of interest in the Holy Spirit, theologians began to analyze its activity in the world. Congar describes the Holy Spirit as the "breath of God in our personal lives . . . " (Vol. I, viii), who is "known to us . . . not directly in himself, but through what he brings about in us." He reminds us that for Augustine, the Spirit "is also at the deepest level the longing that impels us toward God and causes us to end in him" (Vol. I, 81). Congar forewarns us, however, that the Holy Spirit is "active in history and causes new and sometimes very confusing things to take place in it" (Vol. I, 115).

Kilian McDonnell identifies "the Spirit as the place of mediation whereby God touches the church and the world and sets them on the road back to God" (8). For him, the Holy Spirit is: the "other hand of God," a hand that provides each person with universal touch, continuously tapping one on the shoulder and pointing the way home.

Moltmann defines the experience of the Spirit as an "awareness of God in, with and beneath the experience of life, which gives us assurances of God's fellowship, friendship and love" (*The Spirit* 17). He tells us that we must recognize and embrace our authentic Self, and awaken within ourselves genuine self-love. "We cannot love ourselves if we don't want to be ourselves but want to be someone else" (*The Source* 63). God loves us as we really are, "not as we would like to be, or don't want to be" (64). The "total Yes to life and the unhindered love of everything living are the first experiences of the Holy Spirit" (85).

Going deeper, Moltmann refers to the Holy Spirit as "God's indwellings" (*The Spirit* 12). The God within calls the individual to wholeness, to transcend the confines of self-interest and to embrace his or her true Self, i.e., the God who dwells within. Jerome Hall, in *We Have the Mind of Christ*, explains Edward J. Kilmartin's thinking about the Holy Spirit. He writes that it is through the sending of the Spirit that the fulfillment of humankind is realized. Human beings, created with an "orientation toward the Transcendent, yearn for the perfect happiness of personal union with God" (134).

Moltmann emphasizes that the indwelling of the Spirit "goes deeper than the conscious level in us" (*The Spirit* 3). We begin to embrace that Spirit and are in God and God is in us "whenever we are wholly there, undividedly present. The mysticism of everyday life is probably the most profound mysticism of all" (211). For Moltmann, the Holy Spirit is the unrestricted presence of God in which our life wakes up. True spirituality is a full and conscious love of life; the total YES to life and the unconditional love of everything living are the first experiences of the Holy Spirit. The more wholly the individual exists the more he or she is able to sense the presence of God, the source of everything living. For Moltmann, "becoming holy means becoming living, and to sanctify means to make alive" (*The Source* 54).

Karl Rahner, in a homily for Pentecost, states that we Christians are afraid of the Holy Spirit. "We want the Spirit therefore in small doses . . . we trust him only insofar as he is expressed in literary form, in law and tradition, in institutions that have proved their worth" (*The Great Church Year* 217). He states that many Christians have not seen any trace of the Holy Spirit in their lives because they look for him "only under explicitly religious labels" (216), under which they have been religiously trained. He tells us to look for signs of "inner freedom in which a person . . . succeeds, without knowing how, in really breaking out of the prison of . . . egoism; [and] . . . possesses that joy which knows no limit; [and] . . . entrusts [oneself] . . . to an ultimate mystery . . . as unity, meaning and love" (216). Rahner believes that when these signs are present, "what we Christians call the Holy Spirit is at work" (216).

For Rahner, the "word of the Holy Spirit is the question to each individual in his irreplaceable uniqueness as to whether he has the courage to venture, to experiment . . . whether he trusts in something which in the last resort cannot be rationally proved, but which is of course supremely rational wisdom — that is, the Holy Spirit" (219); and which will "lead us into God's eternal life and light" (220).

Bernd Jochen Hilberath, in an essay in *Advents of the Spirit*, writes that the Holy Spirit, as person in the Trinity, is that which we seek to bring about in our own lives: identity through self-transcendence. The Spirit hides, advances, and retreats revealing itself, "as one who by withdrawal allows others to come to the fore" (267). Hilberath argues that "those responsible for the pneumatological deficit, or rather the domestication of the Spirit in the church and in theology," have been unable to experience self-transcendence (267). They fear that in transcending the self, one's identity is lost. Rather than losing one's identity, however, the "Spirit reveals to created spirit — what it means to acquire and preserve one's identity: through self-transcendence, through reaching beyond self to others" (267).

The Holy Spirit calls us to wholeness through self-transcendence: when one reaches beyond oneself to others, one comes to one's true Self. It is through the love that exists in that space of self-transcendence that one's true Self embraces the Self of God and experiences the beginnings of wholeness. The holy and healing work of the Holy Spirit is to lead us to self-transcendence. Within the Trinity, Hilberath explains, the Holy Spirit is the "event of loving encounter, the space into which Father and Son transcend themselves" and are bound together in love into unity (282). It is this "self-transcendence of God in his creative Spirit [that] makes possible the self-transcendence of human beings toward fellow creatures and toward the Creator" (270). Hilberath elaborates that self-transcendence has "its ultimate ground in the conviction that every human being is called by God into existence, addressed by him, animated by the breath of his Spirit, and called to fulfillment through the encounter with him" (283). It is the Holy Spirit who opens up the space and creates the bridge for this loving encounter; it is the Holy Spirit who unites the soul with God (286).

For nearly two millennia Christian theology has seen the Holy Spirit as the expression of God's presence and activity in the world guiding human beings into an eternal loving union with their Creator. From Irenaeus' image of the theatrical producer, to Symeon's heartfelt emotion of being rescued from the swamp; from the mystics' inward experience of being loved, to Moltmann's realization that the Spirit permeates the unconscious to give new life, the work of the Holy Spirit has always been seen to create in the deepest level of the individual soul what Augustine understood to be "the longing that impels us toward God and causes us to end in him" (Congar Vol. I, viii).

The Phenomenon of Synchronicity

Twentieth Century Jungian Insights

Carl Gustav Jung is referred to as the father of analytical psychology. Within his wide spectrum of psychological thought, he is perhaps best known for his theories about integration of the human psyche, the collective unconscious, and synchronicity. Jung gave the world word associations that are used in personality tests, and the concepts of complexes, archetypes, personality typologies, introvert and extrovert. In Deidre Bair's biography, Jung is described as "a psychoanalyst who never underwent formal analysis but used instead his 'personal myth' as the starting point to formulate what he believed were enduring objective truths" (5). The centerpiece of his life work is his theory of individuation, what Bair refers to as "the coming to terms with oneself and one's life" (5).

Jung was born in 1875 into the family of a Swiss Protestant minister. He contemplated entering the ministry but eventually choose a career in medicine. From his childhood, Jung was drawn to questions dealing with spirituality and religion. He pursued psychiatry and psychology under Sigmund Freud and had, early in his career, been considered Freud's chosen disciple to carry on his work in depth psychology. However, Jung eventually broke with Freud over the latter's insistence that all neuroses were the result of repressed sexuality. Freud reduced every psychological process to material causation with its "genesis in infantile sexuality" (Lammers 75). Jung, on the other hand, understood instinctual drives, including sexuality, as "symbols of spiritual forces conducive to health" (75). Where Freud's theory of psychology was based on causation in matter, Jung's was goal-oriented, the goal being psychological and spiritual wholeness.

Individuation: the Drive to Wholeness

Throughout his writings, the topic that most interested Jung was what Robert Aziz describes as the individual's "quest for a highly personalized experience of wholeness" (10). Jung viewed religion as the expression of that quest which he connected with a direct relationship to the "spontaneous manifestations of the unconscious" (11). Aziz quotes Jung to support his point: "The religious need longs for wholeness, and therefore lays hold of the images of wholeness offered by the unconscious, which, independently of the conscious mind, rise up from the depths of our psychic nature" (11). In Jungian theory, the collective unconscious, integration within the human psyche, and the awareness of synchronicity as purposeful messages from the unconscious, were constructs and processes that facilitated that wholeness.

Jung argued that the human individual is teleologically driven; and that the development of the personality, the individuation process, is an unfolding from within the individual in accord with a teleological design of the universe; a design that hard-wires a seed inside of every organism calling that organism to a final purpose. Hall and Norby's *A Primer of Jungian Psychology* describes the individual as beginning life in a "state of undifferentiated wholeness" (81). Mirroring the seed that grows into a plant, the individual is then driven to develop into a "fully differentiated, balanced and unified personality" (81). To Jung that seed is the Self; to Christians it is the soul.

Jung held that causality and teleology are partial principles in harmony with each other, "the soul is teleological in its operation while the body follows causality" (Progoff, *Jung* 72). He argued that "Body and soul subsist together as parts of a pattern that is [and reflects] the universe as a whole" (73). His research led him to identify synchronicity as the vehicle for recognizing that pattern. Jung was not the first to understand this pattern; both Leibniz's concept of 'laws of efficient causes' and Lao Tzu's 'Tao' are "forerunners and sources of his conception of Synchronicity" (75). Leibniz, looking from the mindset of Western thought, sought to "grasp the pattern of these elusive relationships and intangible influences in order to hold firmly in his mind" (75). Lao Tzu, with an Eastern perspective, did not seek to grasp it "but to become part of it, to enter into the movement of the patternings of time that comprise the harmonious flow of nature" (75).

Jung's body of work rests on his principle of individuation, the teleological instinct or drive within the person to wholeness. Ira Progoff, one of the foremost interpreters of Jung's work and a leader in the movement for spiritual transformation, has written that "out of the problems that teleology suggested but could not answer, he [Jung] was led to Synchronicity" (66). Progoff maintains that "the teleological point of view retains the pivotal position in his thinking because it contains cause and effect within it and yet leads directly into the issues of synchronicity" (66). The psyche responds to an innate religious need for wholeness; and to fulfill that need it is necessary that one must become conscious of wholeness, not merely within the psyche but present within the universe and seen through the synchronistic patterning of events in one's environment.

The Collective Unconscious: the God Within

Jung held that there is a dimension of human experience within each individual that both "reflects a depth in us as human beings and also a depth of the universe" as a whole (Progoff, *Jung* 13). At this depth the human psyche "contains reflections of the larger universe" (78); reflections within the microcosm of the individual that take the form of images that symbolically represent universal aspects of the macrocosm. Jung held that these images in the psyche are "reflections of the universe in miniature" (78). He maintains that "The Self of the individual, which means the individuated totality of the person, is then a reflection of the cosmos as a whole" (82).

Robert Aziz in *C. G. Jung's Psychology of Religion and Synchronicity* writes that "For Jung, spiritual wholeness arises primarily out of one's unique and highly personalized encounter with the unconscious" (40). Jung held that through the unconscious the individual is "coextensive with the totality" of the cosmos; and that there exists, in the deepest levels of the psyche, "the presence of an absolute knowledge" as it moves into consciousness and provides the individual with "insights into the events of outer reality, past, present, and future" (111). In his early years Jung saw religious images as arising from a "strictly intrapsychic ground" (180) within the individual. Towards the end of his life, however, he came to view these religious contents as arising from a "universal substrate present in the environment . . . from the transcendental world of the psychoid archetype" (180).

Writing on Jung's theory of the collective unconscious, Father Victor White argues that where the "realm of consciousness is invariably individual, ego-centered: the realm of unconsciousness is supra-individual" (30). The unconscious is always awake and operating. It is "untiring and sleepless (and in this respect also, godlike): unlike consciousness it is unfettered by the categories of space and time, . . . unknown and unknowable to consciousness, it can be known only by its effects as perceived by consciousness. It is itself unfathomable, immeasurable, infinite" (30).

In *Memories, Dreams and Reflections*, Jung maintains that the psyche mirrors the structure of the universe. He holds that whatever happens "in the macrocosm likewise happens in the infinitesimal and most subjective reaches of the psyche." He states that where he prefers the term 'the unconscious,' he might "equally well speak of 'God'." Jung reveals that for him, "it is not that God is a myth, but that myth is the revelation of a divine life in man. It is not we who invent myth; rather it speaks to us as a Word of God" (335–340).

In his essay "A Psychological Approach to the Trinity," Jung argues that the theological statement that dogmas are inspired by the Holy Spirit indicates that they are "not the product of conscious cogitation and speculation but are motivated from sources outside consciousness and possibly even outside man" (150). He sees that religious statements of this kind are the "rule in archetypal experiences and are constantly associated with the sensed presence of numen" (150).

Jung is described in *The Catholic Encyclopedia* as emphasizing "the symbolic, clusters of (complex) associations, psychological types, forms of the subconscious and archetypes" (725). In his studies of Catholicism and, in particular, the Trinity, he found expressions of what he believed to be the collective unconscious. As a student he researched spiritualistic phenomena and observed their similarities not only to Swiss folktales which he had heard since childhood, but to similar folklore and legends that he found were common to cultures around the world and throughout history. His conclusion was that these tales were not merely the product of local superstition but rather connected with "the objective behavior of the psyche" (Jung, *The Portable Jung* ix).

Jung found rich expressions of the collective unconscious in religion. In *Jung and the Bible*, Rollins states that Jung looked at "Scripture as a treasury of the soul . . . the testimony of our spiritual ancestors proclaiming in history and law, prophecy and psalm, gospel and epistle, genealogy and apocalypse, their experience of the holy, and drawing us and others through us into that experience" (v). Jung analyzed Scripture through the lens of his concepts of the soul's process of individuation, the collective unconscious, its central archetype which he named the Self, and the emergence of the Self as the God-within each individual. Jung maintained that "the goal of Scripture is not just to describe God, . . . [but] to point to the One who is at the center of all being, the 'circle whose center is everywhere but whose circumference is unlimited' " (127). Jung saw Scripture as the tutor of the soul in God-consciousness, its purpose being "to bring its readers into the presence of the holy" (127). Jung held that religious symbols and God-images, such as those found in Scripture, are expressions of a central archetype present within the individual. That archetype, the Self, mirrors the "immenseness of the mystery from which we are born, the heights to which we might aspire, and the depths we may have to plumb for the Self to come into its own" (85). Within every single human being "there is an ever-present archetype of wholeness which may easily disappear from the purview of consciousness or may never be perceived at all unless it is awakened and illumined" (86). The image of Christ exemplifies the archetype of the Self. Jung suggests that Jesus Christ "occasions such an awakening and illumining by imparting to the waiting 'soul' an image of that Self for which it has always been longing" (86). Jung believed that the appearance of Jesus on the stage of history "expressed something . . . that was alive and at work within the soul. The good news spread because there was a psychic readiness to receive it" (90). The combination of the ministry of the historical Jesus of Nazareth, the soul's readiness to perceive and interpret him as the Christ, and the activity of the Christian community that subsequently changed the course of history, represented for Jung a prime example of synchronicity.

Ann Conrad Lammers, in *In God's Shadow: The Collaboration of Victor White and C. G. Jung,* summarizes Jung's insights into the drive toward wholeness: the psyche, on its teleological, goal-oriented path to realize its potential wholeness, moves and balances itself within the "tension and ongoing play between ego-consciousness and the unconscious, . . . [seeking] consciously and unconsciously, to develop its potential wholeness" (227). Lammers writes about Jung's affinity for Catholicism: Jung often stated that "only Catholics understood his work on the soul" (133). She maintains that Jung was heavily influenced by Catholic theology and that his concept of the Self came into focus through his analysis of the Trinity and the "symbolic meaning of the Christ-image in Western culture" (154). But the major role in the individuation process was given to the Holy Spirit, whom Jung identified as the "very principle of psychic wholeness and the bridge between human experience and the Godhead" (162).

Synchronicity

In *Synchronicity: An Acausal Connecting Principle*, Jung elucidates his concept of synchronicity: it is the "meaningful coincidence of two or more events, where something other than the probability of chance is involved" (104). Jung held that there are events which are meaningfully related to one another without any possibility of proving that this relation is a causal one. Rather than cause and effect, it is the case of a "falling together in time, a kind of simultaneity" (19). Because of this quality of simultaneity, Jung developed the term 'synchronicity' to "designate a hypothetical factor equal in rank to causality as a principle of explanation" (19). In the phenomenon of synchronicity there is a coming together of what appears to be chance factors, not causally linked, that prove themselves to be meaningfully related and "at the very heart of the process by which the purpose of the individual's life unfolds and becomes his 'fate' " (Progoff, *Jung* 64).

In *The Tao of Psychology: Synchronicity and the Self*, Jean Shinoda Bolen argues that there are interrelationships between the meaningful coincidences of synchronicity and the intuitive sense that we are part of some deep oneness with the universe. She relates the Chinese concept of Tao with Jung's concept of synchronicity, and holds that "synchronicity is equivalent to the Tao" (xii). Bolen reminds the reader that Jung saw the collective unconscious as behaving "as if it were one and not as if it was split into many individuals" (20). Each synchronistic event is a clue "intimating the possibility that we and everything in the universe might be invisibly linked rather than unrelated and separate" (36). To Jung this was evidence for the existence of an "underlying matrix or Tao" (36). Bolen holds that for synchronicity to happen, "the space between individuals and things, rather than being empty, must somehow 'contain' a connecting link or be a transmission medium" (36). This underlying matrix, this connecting link is what Jung called the collective unconscious.

Explaining Jung's concept of synchronicity, Robert Aziz writes that the religious instinct within the individual longs for wholeness. That "wholeness to which one must open oneself is a wholeness that is not only transmitted intrapsychically, but transmitted to the individual through the synchronistic patterning of events in one's environment" (168). This patterning presents meaning; and that meaning "could exist outside the psyche" (174). Jung held that "one and the same (transcendental) meaning might manifest itself simultaneously in the human psyche and in the arrangement of an external and independent event" (174).

Marie-Louise von Franz, a colleague of Jung's for many years, states that in his theory of synchronicity, Jung stressed the point that "since the physical and the psychic realms coincide within the synchronistic event, there must be somewhere or somehow a unitarian reality" (98). To this "reality of the physical and the psychic realms" Jung gave the name *unus mundus*, the one world (98). Jung held that this is a world which we cannot visualize, one that "completely transcends our conscious grasp" (98). He believed that this psycho-physical reality manifests itself to the individual in the synchronistic event.

M. Scott Peck, in his popular classic *The Road Less Traveled*, held that the commonality of synchronistic experiences are indications that "these phenomena are part of or manifestations of a single phenomenon: a powerful force originating outside of human consciousness which nurtures the spiritual growth of human beings" (260).

Across the spectrum of literature surrounding the phenomenon of synchronicity, psychologists, philosophers, and scientists have posited that every living being is part of a whole which is greater than the sum of its parts. Science names this perspective quantum theory. There is a common discernment among the authors researched that all life is connected and interwoven; that everything in the universe is interdependent; and that individual experiences of meaningful coincidences are more than the initial, external impression human beings perceive them to be. Thinkers from Jung to Peck to O'Murchu theorize that human beings experience life not in isolated segments, but in wholes; that there is a unifying principle at work in the cosmos; and that synchronistic experiences are manifestations of a powerful force originating outside of human consciousness which nurtures the spiritual growth of human beings.

Father Diarmuid O'Murchu in *Quantum Theology: Spiritual Implications of the New Physics* reminds the reader that Einstein's theory of relativity proved that "time and space are not two separate entities, but that together they form a space-time continuum, and that energy and mass are, in fact, two aspects of the same phenomenon" (26). This theory holds that things can be "understood only relative (i.e., in relation) to each other, not independent of, nor isolated from, each other, as absolute values" (26). In a quantum universe, "all life operates within the context of relational interaction" (34). O'Murchu uses the human body as "a prime example of quantum theory at work: it is highly complex, yet exhibits an amazing sense or order, rhythm, and purpose" (35). Quantum theory illustrates that the whole is greater than the sum of its parts, and this whole "underpins all reality" (35). O'Murchu echoes Jung to argue that "there is a unifying principle that links the macro and the micro, across the aeons, and throughout the infinity of our universal potential, what Christians traditionally have called the 'Holy Spirit' " (192).

For Progoff, Jung's theory of synchronicity provides a means by which we can "perceive and experience the correlations between the large patterns of the universe and the destiny of the individual" (*Jung*, 148). Progoff held that synchronicity helps us "perceive the movement of life in the universe as that movement is reflected in the life of human beings" (*Jung*, 149).

Illuminating the Promptings of the Holy Spirit

For Jung the Self is the central archetype within the unconscious, the God within us. It is through the individuation process that the human psyche responds to an innate religious need for wholeness. To fulfill that need, the individual must become conscious of wholeness, not only within the psyche but as existing within the universe and discernible through the synchronistic patterning of events in his or her environment.

Catholic theologians such as Victor White discern that the unconscious is in fact the locus of God within us. They understand synchronistic experiences as emanating from the Holy Spirit, God's presence which resides within and calls each of us to wholeness. Each synchronistic event awakens us to the reality that everything in the universe is linked rather than separate. Synchronistic events that occur throughout our life create a 'highway' on which the Holy Spirit travels to reach and guide us. God has sent the Spirit of his Son into our hearts to be a guiding force in our lives, calling us to wholeness through a Self-awareness made manifest in the phenomenon of synchronicity.

Contemporary philosophers, psychologists and religious writers, influenced by Jung, have addressed the efficacy of synchronicity in discerning God's presence and in leading one to wholeness. Today, in every corner of the world, people are graced with glimpses of what Phil Cousineau calls the 'soul moments' in life: moments that have grown to become significant moments in their own soul's journey. It is in these moments of synchronicity that people realize their "connection to the great web of life" (xvi), and that a higher, cosmic power is at work in their lives. Cousineau states that the Jewish skullcap is sometimes seen as protection "against too heavy a message from God" (xvii). Squire Rushnell refers to synchronistic events as 'God Winks,' "little messages to the soul" on the journey through life, nudging the individual along the grand path that has been designed for him or her by God (xiii).

Charlene Belitz and Meg Lundstrom interviewed over fifty people and documented personal stories of synchronicity in *The Power of Flow: Practical Ways to Transform Your Life with Meaningful Coincidence*. Their research underscores the interrelationship between synchronicity and the intuitive sense that we are part of a deep oneness within the universe. They conclude that synchronicity pushes us toward individuation "by speaking to us in ways we uniquely understand, with layers of meaning and resonance that apply to our own lives and no one else's" (28). One's experience of synchronicity intuitively confirms that everything in the universe is linked rather than separate. This link is what Jung calls our collective unconscious, and Christians call God.

In this literature review, parallels were found between the language and metaphors used by Christian Spirit theology and by Jungian depth psychology to describe human spiritual development. Present in both is recognition that human beings are driven, prompted, or called, to what twentieth century depth psychology idealizes as a state of psychological wholeness and names individuation; and what twenty centuries of Christianity understands as a state of spiritual holiness and has named sanctification.

The paths toward individuation and sanctification run side by side — for a while. Individuation may be seen as a secular analogy for sanctification. However, individuation is in many ways self-serving and limited to (and within) the individual, while sanctification is God-serving and continues on for eternity. Nevertheless, the literature speaks to a common light shining on the path to both states: an intuitive sense of being led to wholeness through the unconscious; a sense that is recognizable in the phenomenon of meaningful coincidences.

The modern twentieth century metaphor of synchronicity describes this age-old phenomenon. Whether we see it present in the mystic's intuitive and loving encounter with his or her God, or in "winks," "little messages," or "soul moments," the literature reviewed begins to support the argument that the Holy Spirit is using this phenomenon to get our attention and guide us home.

Chapter Three: Synchronicity Analyzed

Down through the ages of Christianity, for nearly two millennia, the Holy Spirit has been seen as guiding the soul to God. The Spirit's work has been described in metaphors that could be understood within the intellectual and cultural limits of each period in history. To Irenaeus the Spirit was a theatrical producer working the stage of history; for Symeon and Catherine it was a hero-rescuer, enabling the soul to pull itself out of the swamp, or inspiring someone to bring help when most needed; and for McDonnell the Spirit is the other hand of God touching the soul. From Augustine to Moltmann the Holy Spirit has been seen as working at the deepest level of the human psyche to push and pull the soul to end in God, to be sanctified.

Before the twentieth century, Christian theology and pastoral ministry possessed limited knowledge of the unconscious mind and its workings. There was no language, no metaphor to describe the phenomenon of synchronicity, those meaningful coincidences on the road to psychological and spiritual wholeness. And yet there was an intuitive sense in the hearts of the faithful that God was at work in their lives. The emergence of Jungian depth psychology provided insights and a language of metaphors for theologians to begin to understand how God's Spirit works through the unconscious. It provided a paradigm to describe the individual's growth towards psychological and spiritual wholeness, and a language to discern meaningful coincidences as leading to that wholeness.

But depth psychology was limited by its secular nature: it only maintained that synchronistic events can lead the individual to psychological integration and wholeness in this life. Looking at the insights and language of secular depth psychology through the eyes of faith, however, one can see that it provides a template which can be extended to discern and illuminate the soul's journey beyond psychological wholeness (individuation) in this life to spiritual wholeness (sanctification) for eternity. Using this template, the theologian and the pastoral minister can understand the phenomenon of synchronicity as the work of the Holy Spirit leading the soul to eternal union with God. With this new intellectual and cultural metaphor now available to residents of the twenty-first century, synchronistic events can be discerned and illuminated as the work of the Holy Spirit.

In analyzing synchronicity, this research examined how this phenomenon, in theory, affects the individual on the journey or passage to wholeness — first within the psyche, then within the soul. Two process models were created side by side to show their similarities: a Jungian model of psychological individuation, and a Christian model of spiritual sanctification. The manner in which the Holy Spirit uses synchronicity in the process of sanctification was analyzed. A third model was constructed, a Christian model with Jungian insights. It shows the limits of individuation, and how the Holy Spirit uses synchronicity to extend it and lead the individual to sanctification.

This analysis went on to identify groups of people in the literature whose experiences could be viewed in terms of Jungian insights; specifically, events or circumstances that might be considered examples of synchronicity. Two groups were identified: Christian saints and mystics, and ordinary twentieth century individuals. Selected experiences were analyzed, including a published case study of Saint Francis of Assisi, along with published anecdotal experiences of modern contemporaries.

Guiding the Individual to Wholeness

In the Psyche

In Jungian theory, the individuation process is driven by psychic energy which originates in a ground of universal wholeness that exists both internal and external to the person and transcends the boundaries of time and space. This energy becomes activated in the psyche when events and/or images, present in the psyche's environment, trigger templates within the collective unconscious. Jung called these templates archetypes. Archetypes are inherited evolutionary templates which, Jung argued, are genetically passed down from primeval ancestors. They are like photographic negatives that were engraved within the brain over millions of years of evolutionary experience. Energy from events and/or images in the environment flow through the archetypes; and, just as developing chemicals flowing through a negative reveal a picture to the eye, the perception of the event or image flowing through the archetype presents an underlying truth to the psyche. Once the perception is presented, however, the psyche has a choice. It can bring into consciousness, recognize, and act upon the meaning of the archetype and the direction it might lead, or the psyche can shield the archetype from consciousness and ignore its meaning.

Jung identified the central archetype as the Self. He described this transcendent archetype as the unifying function that draws the psyche to wholeness. Once triggered within the unconscious by a synchronistic event, the archetype of the Self has the potential of entering into consciousness and thereby drawing the psyche towards integration and wholeness. Potential becomes reality as the psyche, over time, recognizes the call to wholeness, reaches from ego, or self-consciousness, to Self and embraces the God within. Jung held that within every human being "there is an ever-present archetype of wholeness which may easily disappear from the purview of consciousness or may never be perceived at all unless it is awakened and illumined" (Rollins 86). He argued that the image of Jesus Christ exemplifies the archetype of the Self and "occasions such an awakening and illumining by imparting to the waiting 'soul' an image of that Self for which it has always been longing" (86).

The teleological design of the psyche and the individuation process cause human beings to long for wholeness. Jung held that "the wholeness to which one must open oneself is a wholeness that is not only transmitted intrapsychically, but transmitted to the individual through the synchronistic patterning of events in one's environment" (Aziz 168). Jung defined synchronicity as the phenomenon by which "one and the same (transcendental) meaning might manifest itself simultaneously in the human psyche and in the arrangement of an external and independent event" (174).

In the Soul

Catholic theology teaches that human beings are created with love by God, called to live in and share that love during life, and to dwell with their loving creator throughout eternity . Each person is sent into life with what Jerome Hall refers to as an "orientation toward the Transcendent" and a yearning for the "perfect happiness of personal union with God" (134). This yearning is at the center of the inherent spiritual nature of the individual, and is the driving force in spiritual growth. For that growth to occur, however, desire for and identification with God, i.e., the Transcendent, must move out of its initial unconscious state and into consciousness, where it can be recognized, embraced, and acted upon by the will.

What Jung describes in psychological terms as individuation may be thought of as a stage towards what Catholic theologians refer to as sanctification: a spiritual process that goes on within the human person, whereby the Holy Spirit brings the innate desire for God into consciousness and leads the soul to recognize and embrace God for eternity. Yves Congar paints a metaphor of the Holy Spirit as the "breath of God in our personal lives" (Vol. I, viii). We come to recognize God's presence by what that breath brings about within us.

The Holy Spirit is God's indwelling presence. Jürgen Moltmann wrote that the Spirit dwells in our hearts beneath our conscious level. This indwelling presence calls each human being to wholeness, to transcend the prison of self-interest, and to embrace his or her true Self: the God who dwells within. The Holy Spirit is the presence of God that wakes us up. Once awakened, the subsequent spiritual development that occurs within the individual results in conscious acts of the will to embrace life and to unconditionally love every living being. For the individual to become holy, he or she must become alive. The more alive, therefore, the more whole one becomes; and the more wholly the individual exists, the more he or she is able to sense and embrace the presence of God, the source of everything living (*The Source* 54).

To become alive and whole one must awaken within oneself not only love of God and love of others, but genuine self-love. This requires that one is able to see God within self as well as within others. Moltmann writes that "We cannot love ourselves if we don't want to be ourselves but want to be someone else." God loves us as we really are, "not as we would like to be, or don't want to be" (*The Source* 63–85).

In many instances, love of self can be more difficult than love of others. Human beings have life experiences stored in their memories like data written on a hard drive. Painful experiences, hurts that scrape away at self-esteem, can be more than one's conscious mind can bear. These experiences can become repressed memories that we bury in a compartment within the psyche, a compartment that Jung named the personal unconscious. Destructive behavior can be driven by negative impulses that arise from repressed memories; emotional and spiritual development can be hindered by these unconscious memories. To cope, one often develops a persona or multiple personae — masks that one shows to the world, and often to oneself; masks that obscure one's true, authentic Self; and in so doing stand in the way of psychological and spiritual wholeness. Genuine, and holy, self-love requires that we remove these masks and love ourselves the way God loves us; not the way we think we should be, or want to be, or that others expect us to be, but as God loves us and calls us to be for eternity.

Because we are human, the path to wholeness and holiness winds through the personal unconscious. The masks that we have learned to use for emotional protection, for survival in a world where we may have been made to feel vulnerable and unlovable, often are obstacles to be negotiated as we move towards wholeness. This can be a frightful journey, but one that can be successfully navigated through prayer, psychotherapy where necessary, and with the wisdom and guidance of a competent spiritual director trained to discern and illuminate the guidance of the Holy Spirit. The role of the spiritual director, trained in Jungian insights and metaphors and capable of discerning and illuminating synchronicity in the practice of spiritual direction, is examined in depth in the following chapter.

Hilberath writes that the Holy Spirit calls us to wholeness through self-transcendence. When one reaches beyond ego to God and others, one comes to one's true Self. It is through the love that exists in that space of self-transcendence that one's true Self embraces the Self of God and experiences the beginnings of wholeness (282); it is in this space that sanctification can begin. Self-transcendence has "its ultimate ground in the conviction that every human being is called by God into existence, addressed by him, animated by the breath of his Spirit, and called to fulfillment through the encounter with him" (283). It is the Holy Spirit who "makes [this encounter] possible and furthers our relation to God" (288).

Congar forewarns that the Holy Spirit is active in history and "causes new and sometimes very confusing things to take place in it" (Vol. I, 115). These things are events, signs and wonders so to speak, which Jung and Peck would classify as synchronicity.

Similarities Between Individuation and Sanctification

The following exhibits represent the similarities between the Jungian model of psychological individuation and the Christian model of sanctification and the place of synchronicity in both.

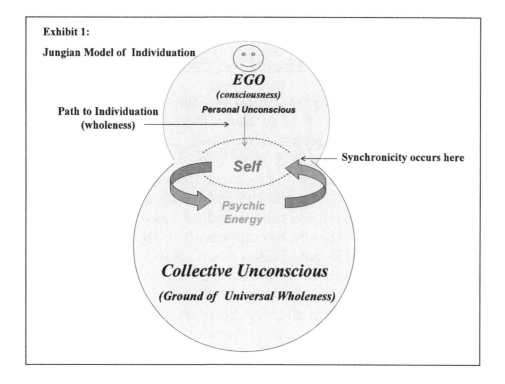

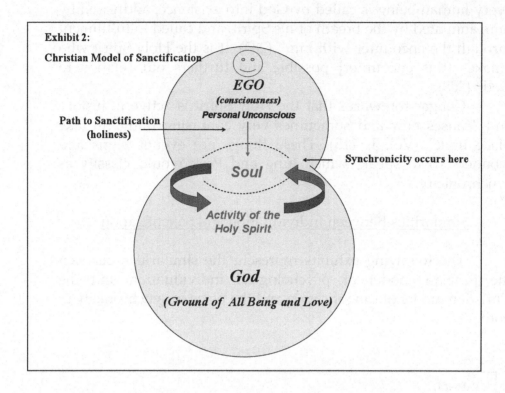

Exhibit 2:
Christian Model of Sanctification

The Holy Spirit as Ringmaster of Sanctification

On the journey to sanctification the individual faces moments of conversion. It is in those moments, those desert experiences when ego defenses come down, that the Holy Spirit can reach and guide, cue and push one to wholeness. Using Jungian insights into the unconscious, the individuation process, and the experience of synchronicity, the pastoral minister can lead others to recognize those cues and pushes as the work of the Holy Spirit, and to ultimately be embraced by God, the source of all wholeness. Brother Donald Bisson describes this recognition as "discernment of freedom for the availability of God" (219).

The trained pastoral minister understands that, as the ringmaster of sanctification, the Holy Spirit uses the experience of synchronicity to reach and guide the soul. On the journey to sanctification there is, using Jungian metaphors, energy released through archetypal activation. This energy can generate synchronistic events that "connect the physical and psychic realms and provide a profound sense of meaningfulness through the overlap of two seemingly disconnected levels of reality" (McMichaels 105). Jungian theory maintains that the unconscious intervenes in the individuation journey. When this intervention occurs, an acausal relationship between the psyche and surrounding physical events presents itself to conscious awareness. This awareness is the phenomenon of synchronicity: a meaningful coincidence "in which external events [or dreams] symbolize what is happening in the psyche" (98). It is the bridge between the unconscious and physical events. The Christian faith teaches that God may intervene in the physical world, interacting with the natural order. The pastoral minister trained in Jungian insights can lead others to discern these synchronistic events as the work of the Holy Spirit, the other hand of God, pointing the way.

The goal of individuation is for the ego to transcend itself, thereby enabling the psyche to embrace its authentic Self. Sanctification does not stop with the individuated, integrated Self. Through its promptings on the road to sanctification, the Holy Spirit leads the individual Self towards integration with the universal Self, God.

The exhibit on the following page represents a Christian model of sanctification with Jungian insights. It shows the limits of individuation, and how the Holy Spirit extends the process beyond those limits into sanctification.

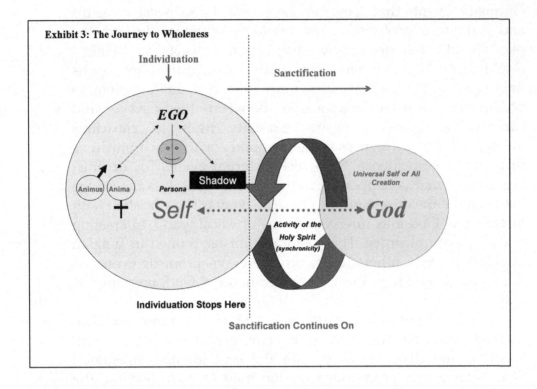

Synchronicity at Work in the Lives of Saints and Mystics

In researching the literature, one finds a relationship between the concepts of depth psychology and the spiritual development of Christian saints and mystics. Jungian insights can add a dimension of understanding and interpretation to the lives of the saints. This is a dimension that Christian theological language alone may not as easily convey to twenty-first century humans, who have been raised in a psychologically attuned culture influenced by Sigmund Freud and Dr. Phil McGraw.

Saint Bonaventure preached that "God is both the essence of each soul and the transcendent goal of the soul's spiritual journey"; that the soul of each individual "is attracted to God transcendent by the God within" (McMichaels 108–109).

Evelyn Underhill analyzed the lives of mystics and wrote extensively on the subject in the early twentieth century. She found that the one common experience shared by all mystics, regardless of religious orientation, was an overwhelming consciousness of God. Underhill argued that spiritual development takes place through the "emergence of intuitions from below the field of consciousness" (Jaoudi 38); that mysticism "is an expression of the innate tendency of the human spirit towards complete harmony with the transcendental order" (Underhill xiv).

Russell Hart, in *Crossing the Border: An Introduction to the Practice of Christian Mysticism*, argues that there is a real world of wholeness accessible within each individual; that although it is perceived dimly, if at all, it is real and immediately present to all who cross an internal border to encounter it. He concludes that Christian mystics are "masters of mystical theology [who] testify to the presence of God within the deepest self" (14).

Maria Jaoudi studied mysticism, and argues in *Christian Mysticism: East and West* that, for the mystic, the universe is a mirror of what already exists in the "eternal now" that is present in everyday life; present "for the looking and seeing through one's inner vision" (4). What Jung calls individuation, Jaoudi sees as the mystic's internal journey to wholeness, and names divinization. Divinization is the process whereby the mystic, through integral intuition, becomes more aware of the presence of God within. The result is such a "deepening awareness that one becomes united to God in and through the realities of life and in one's own thinking, being, feeling, breathing" (38). Jaoudi describes wholeness as "finding one's center and remaining there as the basis of spiritual growth" (24). She cites Eastern Christian tradition, as exemplified by Symeon the New Theologian (eleventh century Greece), and quotes from Symeon's own words, " 'God whose providence extends to all details, how is God not in everything? How is God not in everyone? Yes, God is in the middle of everything. Yes, God is also outside everything'." Symeon taught the many people who came to him for spiritual direction that the way to wholeness is through " 'the illumination of the Spirit' " (44).

In 1957, Ira Progoff, a major interpreter of Jung's work and a leader in the movement for spiritual transformation, translated and wrote a commentary on *The Cloud of Unknowing*, the fourteenth century classic by an anonymous monk. Progoff's purpose was to relate the symbols and concepts contained in this medieval spiritual classic to the "new insights emerging from the study of depth psychology" (*The Cloud* 2). He states that underneath what appear to be vast differences between how the medieval and the modern mindset view the universe and its place within it, there is an "underlying sameness of searching and experience" of wholeness (3). Progoff argues that the *Cloud* describes a state of spiritual development in which the individual is God, and God is the individual "even if only for the briefest atom of a moment" (37). It is at that moment that the individual, having overcome all attachments of the ego and distractions "of any kind [that] may press upon the cloud of unknowing," reaches the "deepest ground of his being," and is no longer just an individual but a participant "in the naked being that is God's ultimate nature" (38).

Saint Francis of Assisi

The relevance of synchronicity to the soul's journey to God is examined in the life of Saint Francis of Assisi. In *Journey out of the Garden*, Susan McMichaels has analyzed Jung's theory of individuation in relation to the spiritual journey of Francis. She argues that both are "complementary visions of the fully realized life" (4); and that Jung's concept of individuation is descriptive of the psychological dimension of Francis' journey, "a restatement, in the language of psychology, of the mystic's journey into identification with the divine" (108). Both Jung's insight into the collective unconscious and the mysticism of Francis share a "commonality of human experience that transcends space and time" (3); and for McMichaels, this validates using twentieth century Jungian language to interpret the thirteenth century life of a saint.

Francis is for Christians "a symbol of our own potential unity with God" (97). Through prayer and meditation, Francis' conscious ego journeyed to awareness of his unconscious Self. This individuation journey of Francis unfolded along what Edward Edinger has named the ego-Self axis. Traveling on this axis "the conscious ego can become aware of the unconscious

Self" (97). This axis is a "channel or conduit that is formed by the ego's willingness to experience messages from the unconscious" (97). McMichaels translates Edinger's metaphor into religious language and names this axis "the power of the Holy Spirit" (97).

McMichaels' argument is that Francis' stigmata was an archetypal expression of the Incarnation, whereby "a transcendent God becomes immanent in creation" (97). Through the stigmata, he experienced God's immanence in his own body. The phenomenon of the stigmata was his willingness to experience messages from his unconscious; it was the "physical manifestation of his psycho-spiritual identification with Christ" (99). In Jungian language, this was an experience of synchronicity; to Christians of faith, it is the work of the Holy Spirit. Through the stigmata, that which emerged from the unconscious, and was identified with by Francis in his conscious mind, represents a miracle. This miracle was that God did "not come down from heaven but emerges from within" his body (111).

As previously noted, archetypal activation generates energy that can result in synchronistic events. These events awaken a profound sense of meaningful coincidence within the consciousness of the individual. The Christian faith teaches that God may intervene in the physical world, by interacting with the natural order. When this intervention occurs, as it did in the case of Francis' stigmata, an acausal relationship between the psyche and surrounding physical events presents itself to conscious awareness. This awareness is the phenomenon of synchronicity; it is the work of the Holy Spirit.

Synchronicity at Work in Ordinary Time

In his foreword to Richard Wilhelm's translation of *I Ching*, Jung writes that "the word synchronicity is applied to what in Taoism is a very ancient concept: the more whole one becomes, the more the ego has been replaced by listening to the Spirit and flowing with the Tao, the more the events in our lives will begin to mirror our internal state" (Jaoudi 43). As he neared the end of his life, Jung understood synchronicity to be the ability to flow with, and discern from, events in our lives; to listen to the Spirit.

He concluded that there was one real world, what he named *unus mundi*, which was behind the reality of everyday life, because human beings experience life not in isolated segments but in wholes; that there is a unifying principle at work in the cosmos; that synchronistic experiences are manifestations of a powerful force originating outside of human consciousness, which nurtures the spiritual growth of human beings. Father Diarmuid O'Murchu is in line with Jung to argue that "there is a unifying principle that links the macro and the micro, across the aeons, and throughout the infinity of our universal potential, what Christians traditionally have called the 'Holy Spirit' " (192).

This unifying principle, this Holy Spirit, is constantly whispering to the individual on many levels. These whisperings can be meaningful coincidences of many kinds that appear to be without cause and defy explanation, dreams that portend an event, and knowledge of events occurring at the same time but in another place. Belitz and Lundstrom, in *The Power of Flow*, describe it "as though the Universe swings into place to give us what we need" (5). Squire Rushnell, as previously mentioned, calls these whisperings 'God Winks'. He makes the analogy to a child at the dinner table with grown-ups, looking up and seeing his or her parent smile and wink. This wink is a sign of loving reassurance. Synchronicity is God's way of establishing a perpetual presence in the life of the individual; of God sending a message of reassurance when it is most needed, perhaps at some crossroads in life, perhaps in times of great uncertainty and instability (4). Synchronicity guides us towards psychological and spiritual wholeness by "speaking to us in ways we uniquely understand, with layers of meaning . . . that apply to our own lives and no one else's" (Belitz 28); through events and dreams that resonate within us and validate our existence; through experiences that lead to self-awareness and self-acceptance, and point the way. To hear these whispers, to see these winks, one need only look in the ordinary time of one's own life.

Baby Kathleen

Belitz and Lundstrom relate the experience of a woman named Beverly Fox Martin of Greenwood Lake, New York. For five long and frustrating years, Ms. Martin tried to adopt an infant daughter. Throughout those years she even had a name for the child she awaited: Kathleen, after her mother. On her mother's birthday, Ms. Martin went to her mother's grave; she asked her to intercede from heaven in her longing for a child. Leaving the cemetery and walking into her home, she heard the phone ring. The call was from the social worker at the adoption agency telling her that an infant girl was available for adoption; the child's birth mother had already given her the name Kathleen (18).

The Brothers Fletcher

Rushnell documents the story of Ron Barren and Roger Mansfield, who were raised within twenty miles of each other in Michigan. Never having met as children, Ron moved to Florida and Roger to Washington state. As adults, both returned at approximately the same time to Michigan; and, coincidentally on the same day, answered the same ad for trainees at The Greenery Nursing Home. They both were hired and sent together to a three week training class at a local community college. After training, they were assigned together to the midnight shift. The men became good friends. One night their supervisor was speaking about the importance of early childhood nurturing. Roger was moved to share his story and told his friends that as a child he had been abandoned. Ron, touched by his friend's openness, shared that he had had the same experience. Both men became engrossed with their similar experiences. Roger mentioned that his birth name was Fletcher. Ron was flabbergasted by this information, because his birth name was Fletcher as well; the two were not only friends but brothers (19).

A Friend Named Fox

I have struggled with doubts that the individual soul survives tragedy and death in an integral state, and that it can know and be reunited with loved ones. Through a powerful experience of synchronicity over a decade ago, these doubts were diminished. This experience involved a dream shortly after the death of a friend named Fox.

Fox was a 45 year old homeless man who lived for nine years at the George Washington Bridge Bus Terminal in New York City. Years earlier he had lost a leg and survived day to day by wheeling his chair in and out of traffic, and up and down subway ramps begging. Over the years, Fox had become a dear friend of mine. I first met him early one Sunday morning when I was bringing coffee and sandwiches to the homeless people who lived alongside the bus terminal. It was winter and I knocked on a large cardboard box and woke him up. I offered him coffee and asked his name. Two weeks later I returned to the terminal. Seeing the same cardboard box with Fox asleep I gently called his name with coffee in hand. He woke up and smiled at me and said, "You remembered my name." My family, as well as many people from our parish, came to know Fox from outreach trips to the bus terminal with food and clothing.

I would see Fox almost every morning as I went to work, and often brought him sandwiches from home. Occasionally after a stressful day at work, I would drag myself up the subway ramp past his wheelchair. Fox would tell me that he was worried about me because I looked so tired. This man who had nothing was worried about me who had so much.

One day I learned that Fox had died in the streets near the terminal of an apparent drug overdose. With the help of the New York City police detectives I was able to locate Fox's body at the City Morgue, where it had been for a month — an unidentified casualty of the streets. His body had been scheduled for cremation on the day prior to my arrival at the morgue, and the coroner was baffled as to why it was still there, as if it were waiting for something or someone.

With the help of our local funeral parlor, I was able to bring Fox's body back to the town in New Jersey where I lived, so that he could be buried with dignity in our parish cemetery. A memorial Mass was celebrated and several people, young and old, who knew him from our outreach team, were present.

An Episcopal Church near the Bus Terminal permitted me to hold a special memorial service for Fox and to invite all the homeless men and women who knew him. At the service one of Fox's friends shared an emotional eulogy: he told us how 'Brother Fox' had given his friends courage and inspiration to take responsibility for building a better life for themselves; how he had been a loving, caring friend; and how much his friends had loved and now missed him.

Several months after Fox's death I had an incredible dream: I was walking in a sunlit meadow filled with beautiful flowers of every color. I heard someone calling my name and in the distance I saw Fox waving to me from his wheelchair. He had a blanket over his lap. As I got closer I heard him shouting, "Lex, Lex, come here, I got something I want to show you!" Fox pulled the blanket off his lap, stood up and danced around with joy. He had two legs and he was whole. I woke from that dream with the most wonderful, peaceful, joyful feeling I have ever experienced.

I believe Fox really came to me in that dream to thank me and give me a gift. It was the gift of showing me that his soul lived on and how much he was loved by God; that despite the circumstances of his death, God had healed Fox, made him whole and welcomed him home. It was Fox's way of telling me through the synchronicity of the dream that everything I believe in is really true; that in the end God finds a way, despite the circumstances of our death, to heal us and make us whole.

Individuation and Sanctification: The Role of Freedom

This chapter has analyzed the theoretical aspects of synchronicity: how it affects the individual on the journey to individuation (psychological wholeness); and how the Holy Spirit works through this phenomenon to guide the individual beyond psychological wholeness to sanctification (spiritual wholeness with God). Though this research maintains that individuation is a stage on the path to sanctification, it is important to recognize the distinction between both, and the reality that a soul can be sanctified without the psyche having attained individuation. Brother Donald Bisson explains that Jung's concept of individuation is a metaphor for the soul's journey to "self knowledge and freedom to respond to God" (147). On this journey, individuation and psychological wholeness are ideals that human beings strive toward, but find difficult to attain. The troublesome person, who struggles through life and alienates others, may not attain psychological wholeness and yet be very close to God, and ultimately reach sanctification. The issue is one of freedom: how much genuine freedom does one have for the journey; and what does the individual do with that freedom? Given the limitations and the degree of real freedom that the individual possesses — as a consequence of psychological, environmental, historical, cultural and biological factors — how loving of God and others was he or she? This is the measure of sanctification.

Karl Rahner argued that there exists within the individual a duality of nature and person. The individual "experiences himself as being at the disposal of other things, a disposal over which he has little control, . . . always conscious of his historical limitations . . . and the contingency of his origins" (*Foundations* 42). Andre Papineau, a Salvatoran priest, author, seminary professor, student of Jungian psychology and long-time friend of the author, interpreted Rahner's view on nature and person for this research. Nature constitutes the givens in life, psychological, physical and social determinants, e.g., our difficult or tragic upbringing by parents, our surroundings that have been supportive or debilitating on our road to maturity. Whereas person represents our potential for becoming what God calls us to be; and is evaluated relative to the degree of freedom our nature allows, and to what extent we are able to handle and overcome the obstacles during life and be kind, gentle and loving in our relationship towards God, others and ourselves. To the extent that we struggle to overcome these obstacles, we may indeed become holy persons even though in our own eyes and the eyes of others we are self-centered and difficult to be with. Given the limits of whatever freedom we do have, we use that freedom to sincerely struggle to become what God calls us to be. We may never psychologically individuate in this life, yet embrace God in sanctification for eternity.

In the following chapter this research analysis unfolds into an examination of an actual pastoral practice, and how the ministry of spiritual direction might use the Jungian insight and language of synchronicity to discern and illuminate the promptings of the Holy Spirit leading directees to healing and wholeness.

Chapter Four: Synchronicity in the Practice of Spiritual Direction

This IPR focused on the experience of synchronicity as the Holy Spirit's activity in one's life, and how insights and metaphors developed by Jungian psychology to describe this experience can be helpful tools in pastoral ministry. Spiritual direction was selected as a specific area of pastoral ministry for analysis. The argument that synchronicity is the work of the Holy Spirit, and the contention that this Jungian insight can help pastoral ministers illuminate and discern the promptings of the Holy Spirit, were examined against the backdrop of an actual practice of spiritual direction that uses Jungian insights — a practice that has been in existence and has grown since the late 1980s.

Research for this chapter is based heavily on the practice of Jungian-based spiritual direction implemented by Brother Donald Bisson, FMS since the 1980s. Brother Donald is a spiritual director, trainer and supervisor of directors. He is widely respected as a commentator and workshop leader on the interrelationship of spirituality and psychology. A Marist brother based in upstate New York, he has graduate degrees in liturgy, spirituality, and transpersonal psychology. His D. Min. was earned at the Pacific School of Religion in the area of Spiritual Direction and Jungian Psychology. Bisson has created a new form of spiritual direction that integrates Jung's metaphor of individuation and the experience of synchronicity with the quest for a deeper life of prayer. He developed this form of spiritual direction in his work with members of an inner city parish in Oakland, California where he lived in the 1980s and early 1990s.

I discovered Brother Donald's work in the course of research for this IPR while searching the Internet for implementations of Jungian analysis in spiritual direction. In addition to researching his writings, interviews and published case studies, I personally entered into spiritual direction with Bisson and have met with him several times at the Marist motherhouse in Esopus, New York.

Ministry of Spiritual Direction

In his doctoral dissertation, "Spiritual Direction and Jungian Analytical Psychology," Brother Donald states that in spiritual direction, the director's ministry is to help directees discern "the movements of God in their lives" (49). Bisson explains that spiritual direction is not psychotherapy or problem-solving for adjustment in society. In direction, it is not the therapist or the director but God who heals and nurtures, sustains, and liberates. Spiritual direction is a "ministry based on real life human experiences, . . . the unique journey of each person within community searching for meaning in the embrace of the unconditional love of God" (63). In this ministry both director and directee become channels of God's love and grace for each other as they work to discern the promptings of the Holy Spirit. They can become conscious of these promptings through recognition and interpretation of synchronistic events.

Catholic tradition has held that prayer, communal liturgy, scripture, counseling, retreats and spiritual reading serve as "major sources of spiritual direction" (McBrien 1214). Bisson holds that "God speaks within the realms of sacraments, prayer, scripture and history <u>and</u> in the human soul" (39). The ministry of the director is "to listen with a discerning heart and mind to the pull of God from the depths [of the soul]" (219). An understanding of insights from Jung's analytical psychology, particularly the phenomenon of synchronicity, can be helpful in this ministry.

The *Harper Collins Encyclopedia of Catholicism* defines spiritual direction as "a guided process of understanding one's relationship with God" (McBrien 1214). It describes the spiritual director as one who listens to both the prayer experiences and the life experiences of his or her directee, and poses meaningful questions to encourage growth and honesty "in facing personal strengths and weaknesses." Spiritual direction is meant to deepen the directee's relationship with God and "raise significant questions about one's spiritual journey" (1214).

Use of Metaphor in Spiritual Direction

Jesuit Father George J. Schemel has written that the evolution of depth psychology that occurred in the twentieth century requires modern spiritual directors to take into account the "place of the unconscious in spiritual direction and in people's lives" (1). Schemel holds that while the traditional practice of spiritual direction focuses on the director's dialogue with the directee's conscious ego, it is important that "we give God not only our ego, what we are aware of, but that we give God our whole self, conscious as well as unconscious"; this will fulfill Jesus' command to love God with our whole soul (6).

Schemel argues that while the terms and metaphors used by Freud and Jung are different, the Christian tradition of spiritual direction has always dealt with the dynamics of the unconscious. He points to Teresa of Avila's metaphor of seven mansions to describe the dialogue between God and the human soul, and John of the Cross's metaphor of active and passive nights, as examples. The Catholic tradition of spirituality has long recognized the "way that God is entering into the lives of people" through the unconscious (6). Schemel holds that while there have been different ways of naming and describing it, the "reality of God entering into a person's life, and that person's responding is basically the same throughout the ages" (2); the experience of this reality as expressed from age to age is always the same: complete union with God. He argues that "one can take various ways that people have of describing that process as a kind of metaphor" (2). Jung's concept of synchronicity is a metaphor for the experience of God's spirit touching one's life.

Italian is a lovely language; so too is Korean. A man in Seoul can passionately describe the beauty of a sunset; a woman in Rome can fill up with emotion witnessing and describing that same sunset. Each, in his or her unique language of symbol and metaphor, would be expressing the same phenomenal experience, and yet so differently expressed; neither would understand the other's expression of the same absolute reality. Bisson explains how metaphor is "transformative language" (6), reflecting indirectly to an experienced reality. In spiritual direction, language and metaphor can never adequately define the soul's absolute experience of and relationship to God. Rather, they are tools that "creatively extend" that experience (6). Both the director and the directee rely on a "common symbol system" (88) to communicate and establish a bond as they walk together on a journey of faith. The absolute that is experienced and communicated is a "living faith" (88). Like the Korean praising the sunset in his native tongue, the director and the directee use metaphor to express encounters with God, the absolute of unconditional love.

Jungian metaphors can be used in today's psychologically attuned society as "tools to express the inner language of the soul" (147). The metaphors of individuation, the collective unconscious, synchronicity, shadow, persona, anima/animus, and Self, can be used to describe the complexity of the inner spiritual journey, and to discern and illuminate the guidance of the Holy Spirit on that journey. Jung's concepts of individuation and synchronicity are metaphors for the soul's journey to "self-knowledge and freedom to respond to God" (147). This complex journey winds through the personal and collective unconscious; it is a journey where the signposts are often meaningful coincidences and dreams. The Jungian insight and metaphor of synchronicity can help the contemporary Christian, enlightened and influenced by knowledge of the unconscious and psychology, to discern the cues and pushes of the Holy Spirit on the journey to wholeness and sanctification.

Role of Spiritual Director in Jungian-based Direction

In his doctoral dissertation, Bisson argues that the integration of "tools and insights gathered from the analytical psychology of Carl Jung" (4) can assist the ministry of spiritual direction to "more effectively transform and reshape the lives of modern Christians" (83). Though enhancing the process and creating a "new vision of the direction ministry" (218), Jungian analysis can never be seen as a replacement for it. The use of Jungian concepts and language in direction by a trained director can "enhance spiritual growth and human development" (33) through the various stages of individuation. Through his or her understanding of Jungian insights, the spiritual director can help the directee to recognize experiences of synchronicity as the promptings of the Holy Spirit on his or her soul's journey. Bisson maintains that guidance of the soul in modern times requires the director to have a "foundational knowledge of the psyche" (29) and an "understanding of the dynamics of the inner life" (89).

John J. Costello wrote about Jung's admiration for the nineteenth century French priest and spiritual director, Henri Huvelin. He notes that Jung's approach as an analytical therapist and Huvelin's as a pastoral minister are similar. The methods used by both to guide those in their care dealt with the content of the unconscious. In both cases the content of the unconscious is the same, and the analyst and the spiritual director are seeking to heal. But the spiritual director goes further "in seeking to sanctify" (Costello 3). The spiritual director differs from the Jungian analyst in a significant way. His or her objective is to use Jungian insights and metaphors to help the directee discern the Spirit's presence and activity leading the way to sanctification.

Bisson recognizes that many look to Jungian theory as a "new mystical system or religious creed" (35), and cautions that an unconditional acceptance of all Jungian presuppositions has the effect of universalizing all religions "into an amorphous new religion, radically individualized and contradictory to traditional faith" (83). He argues that Jungian-based spiritual direction rests on the "need for relationship with the unconscious on our journey with and to God" (84) and the usefulness of Jungian insights in facilitating that relationship.

More than possessing an intellectual understanding of Jungian concepts, the director must be competent to interpret and integrate those concepts into the ministry and process of direction. To do this, he or she must be open "to working with materials from the unconscious as an element within spiritual direction" (82). Bisson holds that this openness creates "harmony between the dual processes of individuation and spiritual growth, psychic and religious experiences, healing and holiness" (82). It empowers the director to minister to the "whole person in the spiritual journey from the outer and inner perspectives" (82). It enables the director to recognize the workings of the Holy Spirit rising from the depths of the psyche.

Jungian Insights Applied to Spiritual Direction

The journey of each individual soul home to God is unique, "yet there are deep archetypal patterns which transcend the details of an individual's life" (14). Bisson argues that by facilitating a "greater dialectic between the conscious and unconscious," (47) the use of Jungian insights and language in spiritual direction aids the Holy Spirit to guide the individual toward healing and wholeness; and to "transcend the alienation and pain of the past into a new synthesis and integration" (47).

The Unconscious

Jung's concept of individuation and its path through the unconscious is important in understanding where synchronicity attempts to lead one, and how the Holy Spirit uses this phenomenon to guide the soul to sanctification and union with God. Bisson, like Schemel, maintains that the discovery of the unconscious has "irrevocably changed the spiritual director's role in the inner journey" (90). The Catholic experience of spiritual direction has traditionally been driven by the connection with the conscious ego of the directee. By introducing Jungian theory into direction, "both the elements of the personal and collective unconscious have been activated" (90), and the ability for the director to see and probe beyond the persona, the mask of the ego, has been enhanced.

Freud saw the unconscious as a personal ontogenetic prison for the psyche and a barrier to sexual adjustment. It was a repository of painful and repressed memories and experiences, creating obstacles for the patient's interaction with others and achievement of social health. Jung, in contrast, recognized that the unconscious was ontogenetic in that it held "repressed or abandoned personal material" (Bisson 34), but also phylogenetic and cosmogenetic in that it contained "the greater collective unconscious" (35). Where Freud's theory of psychology was based on causation in matter, Jung's was teleological; the goal being psychological and spiritual wholeness. To achieve this wholeness, the spiritual director, using Jungian tools, helps the directee to recognize the promptings of the Holy Spirit in synchronistic events and dreams. This illumination of the Spirit at work opens channels within the psyche that "release energy for transformation" (91) and help the directee to "withdraw the projections from the demons within or without" (91), recognize, befriend and own the different elements within his or her psyche; and that ultimately free the directee to receive the Spirit's healing. This transforming energy of synchronicity enables the soul to move forward towards spiritual wholeness.

Individuation and Conversion

The goal of Jung's individuation process and the goal of Christian conversion are similar: "a new integration, a recreation of one's orientation to life" (111). In the first meeting that I had with Brother Donald Bisson, he explained that the experience of synchronicity and the process that Jung called individuation can be thought of as ways in which God uses cycles of conversion during the course of the soul's journey through life to keep turning the soul more consciously towards God. For the Christian, each conversion experience is one of the "key moments in the lifelong process of becoming whole" (128), and going home to God. For Jung, individuation is the process through which the individual consciously grows to recognize and become his or her true, unique and complete Self; and the experience of synchronicity illuminates the way. Individuation is the result of many cycles of conversion, "a lifelong struggle and movement towards wholeness with recognition of a transcendent function operating within us" (110). On the journey to sanctification the Holy Spirit uses the experience of synchronicity to lead the individual to recognize that transcendent function Christians know as God. This recognition is never complete during life; it is an ongoing cycle of conversion and metanoia that ultimately brings the soul back home to rest in God for all eternity.

Schemel, like Jung, maintains that dealing with the unconscious is "the task of the second half of life" (6). During the first half of life the individual's focus is on development of the ego and its associated persona. This focus enables the individual to create a social identity; this social identity allows one to obtain an education, choose a vocation, raise a family, advance in career and become a contributing member of society. Schemel states that mid-life begins for many modern individuals "about ten to fifteen years after a major commitment", putting them into the "mid-thirties or forties" (6).

In mid-life the identity one has created often comes into question and the ego experiences dissonance: the person one thought himself or herself to be becomes challenged by life experience, behavior, loss and broken relationships. Bisson states that it is at this point that many people begin spiritual direction; the point where they discover "their ordinary lives radically changed and surrounded on all sides by desert" (24). Schemel likens this to a "Descent into Hell, . . . the Holy Saturday experience" (13). This, paradoxically, is the most fertile point in one's life to begin integrating the unconscious. It is in those moments, those desert experiences when ego defenses come down, that the Holy Spirit can reach and guide, cue and push one to wholeness. Using Jungian insights into the unconscious and synchronicity, the trained spiritual director can help the directee interpret those cues and pushes as the work of the Holy Spirit and recognize one's authentic Self, and to ultimately be embraced by God, the source of all wholeness. In our first direction session, Brother Donald described this recognition as "discernment of freedom for the availability of God." The spiritual director, using Jungian insights and metaphors, leads the directee to recognize and interpret synchronistic experiences and dreams as the "other hand of God," the Holy Spirit, guiding the soul through the desert to conversion.

Obstacles to the Work of the Holy Spirit

Jungian psychology maintains that projections are defense mechanisms, or compensations, for ego consciousness. By understanding and interpreting these phenomena, the deep feelings and longings of the directee can be illuminated, and the promptings of the Holy Spirit at the base of the Self, the soul, can more easily be discerned. Jung developed metaphors to describe projections of the psyche that must be recognized and integrated for wholeness to unfold. These projections stand in the way of psychological and spiritual wholeness, and can blind one to the Spirit's work. Jung metaphorically named these the shadow, and the animus and the anima (i.e., the contra sexual aspects of one's personality). The process of Jungian-based spiritual direction leads to recognizing these projections and integrating them within one's authentic Self. This process necessitates facing one's shadow and integrating with the contra sexual aspects of one's personality, i.e., one's animus or anima. To face one's shadow and to integrate one's contra sexual personality, one must withdraw projections both negative and positive from oneself, from God and from others; by so doing "we become psychologically whole and unique" (Bisson 43).

Where the Self is the center of the total individual, the ego is the center of consciousness. As previously noted, the individual, during the first half of life, develops a mask or persona in order to embrace a role or position in society. As part of this masking, the ego denies possessing qualities or attributes that are considered to be inferior within the value system associated with its persona. These qualities or attributes cannot simply be eliminated from consciousness, so the ego projects them: they form a shadow that projects outward onto others. In the second half of life, the individual finds himself or herself in the desert and seeks analysis and/or spiritual direction; "the first inner character to challenge our self-knowledge is the shadow" (43). The shadow is "threatening [to the ego] because it carries the inferior characteristics and repressed material of the person" (43). Bisson states that the shadow is not necessarily evil; it is the dark side of our personality that comprises "the unlived, repressed and rejected part of our personality" (122). It often reflects untapped potential that could help the individual cope with the challenges and losses of life. To more clearly see the work of the Holy Spirit leading one to wholeness, the projection of the shadow must be withdrawn from others and assimilated as part of the authentic Self. The director trained in Jungian insights can facilitate this assimilation. Withdrawing projections "demands a sacrificial stance by the ego for the sake of the transformation of the whole psyche" (42). In order for one to consciously withdraw a projection, one must be willing to accept that an unconscious quality of one's own has been attributed to another. Bisson acknowledges that it "requires a unique moral kind of stamina to carry one's own garbage and not dump onto others" (44).

Continued repression makes it difficult for one to discern the prompts of the Holy Spirit and will inhibit spiritual growth; "for the shadow will emerge unconsciously by slips of the tongue, nightmares, and a general sense of not being grounded or real" (122). The shadow must "be recognized and invited to be a companion on the journey"; its integration demands the conscious discerning of the differences between "good and evil, brokenness and healing, health and sickness" (122).

Jung held that men and women have contra sexual aspects of their personalities. A man has a secondary feminine nature; conversely, a woman a secondary masculine nature. In the first half of life these contra sexual aspects of one's personality are projected outward onto members of the opposite sex. Identifying with the opposite sex causes anxiety in the developing ego; so, as with the shadow, these contra sexual qualities are projected outward. Individuation requires that one withdraw these projections and assimilate them into the whole of one's conscious identity; recognizing and embracing them as aspects of the authentic Self. Bisson maintains that in Jungian-based spiritual direction, the man is guided to withdraw "the projected anima from the woman of his life and grows in interior freedom as well as becoming a more responsible adult. So too, a woman withdraws her projected animus from an outer male in order to grow in consciousness" (124). This enables the individual to assimilate the contra sexual part of his or her nature and to perceive the person with whom they share an intimate relationship as a true and separate self, rather than a projection of oneself. This is important because the Holy Spirit is often working within the loving relationship of two people. The assimilation of one's contra sexual identity removes the obstacles created by projection and makes it easier to discern the Spirit at work within the relationship.

Bisson defines the Self as the "archetypal image of man's fullest potential and the unity of the personality as a whole" (234). It is the Self, not the ego, that is the center of the total psyche; it is the Self that intuits and responds to the Holy Spirit's use of synchronicity. The individuated Self encompasses the fullness of the personality by assimilating projections and unifying opposites. For the Christian, the authentic Self is the soul, a microcosm within the individual that is called to embrace and be embraced by God, the macrocosm of universal Self. In the last stage of Jungian-based spiritual direction, what Jung called individuation, there is the experience of the encounter between the individual's authentic Self and God, the universal Self, who is "the center of all that is conscious and unconscious" (125).

Synchronicity in Spiritual Direction

For Christians, the Holy Spirit is the ringmaster of sanctification. Spiritual direction based on Jungian insights calls one to transcend ego and embrace one's authentic Self, and ultimately to be sanctified. It is through the love that exists in that space of self-transcendence that one's true Self encounters and embraces the Self of God, and experiences the beginnings of wholeness. It is the Holy Spirit, the other hand of God, who works in this space to prompt and lead us, and who "makes [this encounter] possible and furthers our relation to God" (Hilberath 288).

During Jungian-based spiritual direction energy is frequently released through archetypal activation. As previously noted, the Holy Spirit uses this energy to generate synchronistic events that link and overlap the physical and psychic realms and create a sense of meaningful coincidence for the director and the directee. The awareness of this experience is the phenomenon of synchronicity: a meaningful coincidence "in which external events or dreams symbolize what is happening in the psyche" (98). The Christian faith teaches that God may intervene in the physical world, interacting with the natural order. Synchronicity is the manifestation of the Holy Spirit's intervention. The spiritual director trained in Jungian analysis can lead the directee to discern these synchronistic events as the work of the Holy Spirit.

Synchronicity and Its Impact

The appendix of this IPR contains a personal reflection that describes a powerful transformative experience of synchronicity; an experience that occurred during research for this project after I began spiritual direction with Brother Donald Bisson. It is included in this IPR not as validation for the research thesis, but as an illustration of the dynamic of synchronicity and its impact on one person's spiritual journey.

Chapter Five: Reflection and Analysis

<u>Insights from this Project</u>

This research has analyzed the experience of synchronicity as the work of the Holy Spirit guiding the soul to healing and wholeness. It has also examined how an understanding of the experience that Jung named 'synchronicity' can be a tool for pastoral ministers to discern and illuminate that work. For the sake of brevity this IPR was entitled, "Synchronicity as the Work of the Holy Spirit." A more accurate title might have been, "Synchronicity is a Twentieth Century Term that Can Meaningfully Describe, to People Who are Attuned to Psychology, the Way in Which the Holy Spirit has Always Worked to Lead Souls to God." But that would be much too long.

This project did not measure quantitative data or involve statistical analysis. It does not deal with an objective reality that is capable of being measured. Rather than attempting to confirm its thesis through deductive reasoning, this IPR takes a qualitative approach and seeks to explore and interpret inductively. Its purpose was twofold. The first objective was to review and integrate two major tracks of literature: the theology of how the Holy Spirit works in the world; and the Jungian concept of synchronicity, and how this concept relates to the integration of the human personality with the goal of spiritual wholeness, and can be used to illuminate the Spirit's work. The second objective was to examine an existing pastoral practice that can support its thesis that the experience Jung named 'synchronicity' is the work of the Holy Spirit, and that this twentieth century Jungian insight and metaphor for an age-old phenomenon can be a helpful tool for pastoral ministry.

Unlike pastoral application projects that are quantitative, the thesis of this pastoral research cannot be proven. It would not be possible to prove that synchronicity is in fact the work of the Holy Spirit; neither is it possible to quantitatively prove that there is in fact a Holy Spirit. What is required in both instances is a qualitative leap of faith. But that leap is not blind; it rests on theology and on a subjective, intuitive sense of a reality that is supported by literature and by an established practice of Jungian-based spiritual direction.

Interpretation, reflection, and analysis of what has been learned in the course of this research focus on these conclusions:

- The Holy Spirit uses the experience of synchronicity to assist in its work of guiding souls to wholeness and union with God.
- The Jungian insight and language of synchronicity is a tool that can assist pastoral ministers to discern and illuminate the Holy Spirit at work in the lives of those to whom they minister.

The Holy Spirit was, for Saint Augustine, "at the deepest level the longing that impels us toward God and causes us to end in him" (Congar Vol. I, 81). For Yves Congar, the Holy Spirit is the "breath of God in our personal lives" (Vol. I, viii). Jürgen Moltmann wrote that the Spirit dwells in our hearts beneath our conscious level. This indwelling presence calls the individual to holiness. This is the sanctifying work of the Holy Spirit: to lead one beyond Self and into the arms of God forever.

The Holy Spirit uses synchronistic experiences to wake us up and send us a message. Synchronistic events create, within the individual, an awareness of meaning and purpose. In Christian theology, it is God who intervenes in the physical world interacting with the natural order to bring about this awareness. The pastoral minister, attuned to synchronicity, can heighten this awareness and enlighten others to discern the cues and pushes of the Holy Spirit. Through prayer and training in Jungian insights, the pastoral minister can guide those in his or her care through the journey of the soul. By illuminating the work of the Holy Spirit, pastoral ministers can enable communication and integration between the conscious and unconscious, and thereby help those under their care toward healing and wholeness.

Implications of Research

For the IPM

This research has repeatedly crossed paths and been integrated with the array of subjects I have studied during the course of graduate work at the IPM. Coursework in Theology, Liturgy, Human Relations in Ministry, Sacraments, Christology, Scripture, Spirituality, and Ecclesiology provided a rich foundation from which to begin discovery of how the Holy Spirit makes its presence known. Of most significance were the theology of the Holy Spirit, the God of Surprises, and the relevance of sacramental signs and symbols as doorways to the sacred, leading the soul to holiness.

An understanding of the significance of meaningful coincidences — the Jungian insight of synchronicity — could be incorporated, albeit briefly, into the IPM syllabus. Such exposure might encourage pastoral ministers to conduct further research into the experience of synchronicity and the relevance of the unconscious for the soul's journey to wholeness. Further study and use of insights provided by Jungian analysis and other depth psychologies could add to the uniqueness of the IPM and its efficacy in preparing well-rounded pastoral ministers to use all the tools that faith and science have at hand.

For Ecclesial Teaching and Pastoral Practice

Vatican II reawakened the consciousness of the Church to the active presence of the Holy Spirit in the world. The Council reminded believers that it is through God's Spirit that Christians are led to truth. Theologians since the Council have urged believers to be receptive to the promptings of the Holy Spirit, while at the same time noting that those promptings are not easy to discern.

Using Jungian insights to illuminate the traditional Christian understanding of the Holy Spirit's activity in the world will benefit the Church in a psychologically attuned twenty-first century society. As has been supported with this research, these insights offer pastoral ministers useful tools for discerning and communicating the presence and the promptings of the Holy Spirit at work in their own lives and in the lives of those to whom they minister. Through spiritual direction, catechesis, preaching, teaching, and small-group sharing, ministers of the Church can employ Jungian language and insights to raise the threshold of personal receptivity to the Holy Spirit's promptings within the community. By so doing, these pastoral ministers may themselves, in effect, become instruments of the Holy Spirit and collaborators in the soul's journey.

For Ministry

As a deacon for thirteen years, I have been fortunate and blessed to share parts of soul journeys with many fellow travelers in several different contexts. Parish ministry has been a constant throughout these years. One dimension of that parish ministry involved initiating and facilitating a support group for adults passing through a desert experience: a time of loss, depression, anxiety. The impetus for pursuing the IPM was a desire to prepare for a full-time second career in pastoral ministry, with a strong interest in ministering to others through counseling and spiritual direction.

I was introduced to the work of Carl Jung during graduate work in psychology in the mid-1970s. Jung's system of analytical psychology resonated with my love for the Eucharist and for my Catholic faith. Over the years, as I read much of Jung's work, I was drawn to his insight into synchronicity. As I experienced synchronicity many times, I came to understand that these experiences were orchestrated by the Holy Spirit to help my soul along the journey home.

My faith journey unfolded through diaconal formation and ministry and led me to the IPM. As all roads are said to lead to Rome, these parallel tracks in my life led me to choose this IPR project. During the course of this project, my interest and insights into the value of Jungian analysis for spiritual direction steadily unfolded. The meaningful coincidence of finding Brother Donald Bisson and beginning spiritual direction enhanced this IPR academic journey into a personal spiritual journey. Both the academic and the spiritual insights received during this journey have enriched my soul. It is my intent to integrate these insights into my diaconal ministry and to pursue training as a spiritual director.

Chapter Six: Future Directions

Contributions of this Research to Pastoral Ministry

This research offers the field of pastoral ministry an understanding of the experience that Jung named 'synchronicity', and it explains how this Jungian insight can be a tool for pastoral ministers to discern and illuminate the work of the Holy Spirit. This research, together with research previously done by Brother Donald Bisson, will, I hope, excite the imagination and prompt pastoral ministers to explore a new frontier in spirituality. This new frontier is the human unconscious. The question for further research is: *How does God use the unconscious to communicate with and sanctify humanity?*

Through his 1990 doctoral dissertation, Bisson enriched the field of pastoral ministry with a vision, new for its time, of integrating spiritual direction with Jung's analytical psychology. By articulating this vision, he opened a window for the direction ministry to take advantage of the positive aspects of Jungian insights, such as synchronicity and individuation, without losing sight of the true purpose of that ministry, i.e., illuminating the presence and promptings of the Holy Spirit. Bisson cautioned those who would pursue his research into the future against "degenerating into a simplistic Jungian interpretation" (219). He reminded his readers that "Christian direction always remains fixed on the Gospel of Jesus Christ, and on the establishment of the reign of God through peace, love and justice" (219). Bisson gave pastoral ministers a challenge to draw on the advances of analytical psychology so that they may "listen with a discerning heart and mind to the pull of God from the depths as well as the community of faith" (219).

As supported by this project, sixteen years after Bisson's pioneering work, Jungian insights offer pastoral ministers useful tools for discerning and communicating the presence and the promptings of the Holy Spirit. These tools are not only useful in the context of spiritual direction, but may be further researched and applied in other areas of pastoral ministry. Through the illumination of the Spirit at work in synchronicity, the pastoral minister, trained in Jungian insights, can guide those with whom he or she ministers to interpret liturgical, sacramental and meditative experiences, as well as to positively address preparatory, transitional and degenerative life experiences. The pastoral minister can listen, interpret synchronistic experiences, and pose meaningful questions. These questions can encourage recognition and withdrawal of shadow and contra sexual projections, and lead to recognizing, accepting and embracing one's authentic Self, as well as the authenticity of others.

Pastoral Areas for Further Research

Geriatric and end-of-life areas of pastoral ministry offer fertile ground for further research and ministerial service. Given the complexities of life, Christians may enter their later years with loneliness and baggage accumulated from a lifetime of self-rejection, never having been good enough, in their own perception, to merit unconditional love. When one is unable to experience self-love, it is difficult to unconditionally love others. Pastoral guidance in recognizing the presence of the Holy Spirit in synchronistic events and dreams can help the aged soul to accept, love, and integrate his or her own shadow, without demanding perfection. This ministry can help the aged and terminally ill soul to find peace within itself and reconciliation with estranged friends and relatives.

People enslaved by addictions, and those suffering from a history of abuse and trauma live in a vicious cycle of self-abuse and self-hatred. Research into the use of Jungian insights as tools for pastoral counseling may prove effective in breaking through the filter of self-hatred. Trained pastoral ministers may be able to help lift the burden of addiction and abuse, and in so doing lead others to break this cycle and find self-acceptance, freedom and peace in the embrace of an unconditionally loving God.

Those incarcerated for failing to integrate into society, and for committing unspeakable acts, are never disowned by God. Often, they disown themselves, closing the window to God's healing grace and redemption. Research into the efficacy of Jungian insights may enable the pastoral minister to lead the prisoner to unlatch that window and slowly open it to God's healing and redemptive love.

Couples meeting with a pastoral minister for marriage preparation, and those who later come for marriage counseling, may have their perceptions and expectations of each other distorted by contra sexual projections. Research into the pastoral use of Jungian insights for marriage preparation and counseling might enable the pastoral minister to help couples recognize and withdraw these projections, integrate them into a mature personal sexual identity, and thereby promote the spiritual and emotional health of the relationship.

Christian spirituality has become popularized through the discipline of Centering Prayer, a method of meditative prayer drawn from the ancient prayer practices of Christian contemplative monks and nuns. These practices were translated in the 1970s and made accessible to all the faithful by three Trappist monks, William Meninger, Basil Pennington and Abbot Thomas Keating at Saint Joseph's Abbey in Spencer, Massachusetts. Research into the potential for synchronicity and active imagination to enrich the practice of Centering Prayer would be an interesting project for pastoral ministers involved in meditative spirituality.

In his 1990 dissertation, Brother Donald Bisson presented a challenging question to future researchers: to what extent are Catholic sacraments and liturgy archetypically based, and how might these rituals help the faithful "deepen their personal and collective roles" in worship (227)? With a modern appreciation for the many dimensions of Christian liturgy and sacraments, pastoral ministers, involved in liturgical planning and direction, might bring benefit to their worship communities by researching the value of synchronicity for understanding and enriching Catholic worship.

Jungian concepts have a close relationship to Eastern philosophy as well as to Christianity. An interesting area for further research would be the applicability of Jungian insights and the patterns of synchronicity manifested in Judaism and Islam.

On to the Future

I have been personally enriched by this research project. In my post-IPR world, I will pursue two applications of this research as personal goals:
- To be trained in the prayerful and effective use of synchronicity in the ministry of spiritual direction, and subsequently to develop a parish-based direction ministry.
- To develop and teach an effective academic course for introducing pastoral ministers to the value of depth psychology and Jungian insights for ministry.

Those attracted to the research and use of depth psychology and Jungian insights in ministry need always remember that ministry is a labor of love — love of God and love of others. Jungian insights and metaphors are only a language, like Italian or Korean. They are helpful in describing and communicating the absolute reality of the soul's journey home to God. As Bisson reminds his readers, the Christian must remain "fixed on the Gospel of Jesus Christ, and on the establishment of the reign of God through peace, love and justice . . . and must listen with a discerning heart and mind to the pull of God from the depths" of the soul (219).

Appendix: A Personal Experience of Synchronicity and Its Impact

What follows is a personal reflection that describes a transformative experience of synchronicity; an experience that occurred during research for this project after I began spiritual direction with Brother Donald Bisson, a religious who is a widely recognized and well-respected pioneer in the use of Jungian insights as a tool for spiritual direction. It is included here as an illustration of the dynamic of synchronicity and its impact on one person's journey.

In the spring of 1987, the archdiocese of Newark, New Jersey was preparing to end its moratorium on classes for new students in diaconal formation. Eleven of us had been tentatively accepted for formation four years earlier and were anxiously waiting the reopening of the gates. For some time I had been struggling with conflict about going forward towards ordination while my sisters in Christ were denied entry; and in that spring, I withdrew my application.

I lived with sadness over this decision for six months. At the end of that time the mother of Michael, one of my TaeKwonDo students, had coincidentally given me a photograph taken on the occasion of her son's promotion test to first degree black belt (Exhibit 4). The photo was taken after my wife and I had performed the symbolic ritual of tying the black belt around Michael's waist. In the photo my hands are on Michael's shoulders and I am smiling into his eyes. Through this photograph, my unconscious was intervening to bring a message into my conscious awareness. Looking at it stirred emotion in me. I did not understand at the time what it was that I saw, but I knew that I was being prompted by the Holy Spirit, doubts and conflict notwithstanding, to return to diaconal formation. This was one of many cycles of conversion turning my consciousness towards God.

Exhibit 4: Michael's Promotion Test

As a person, a husband, a father and a deacon, I have struggled with a lifelong sorrow: both of my parents have suffered from emotional illness. A veteran of combat in World War II, my dad committed himself to an institution for life when I was three years old. My parents separated. My dad was lobotomized, and I didn't see him again until I was in my teens, shortly before he died. My mom suffered greatly with anxiety and depression. As children often do, I felt responsible for my parents' pain and suffering. No matter what success I achieved throughout life, in my mind I was always a failure, a fraud. I was the little boy who wasn't good enough to save his dad, the teenager and adult who couldn't save and bring happiness and peace to his mom.

My life journey has been blessed: a wonderful marriage to my high school sweetheart, who, throughout forty years, has always been my best friend and lover; the gift of four souls, our children, to help prepare for lives and loves of their own; a fulfilling career. But in my mind, I was always the great impostor, a con man, a fraud. Throughout my life, when facing stressful periods, I would have a recurring dream: I would be sitting on a toilet, in a public area; with people watching, as I was unable to clean myself.

As a deacon, a powerful image came through in my active imagination: it was the image of Jesus meeting a soul at death; welcoming into eternity, and embracing that soul while saying the words, 'Welcome home, my beloved child.' It was an image I used in homily after homily, for funerals, baptisms and weddings, to express the journey of the soul and its fulfillment in the embrace of the unconditional love of God. Twelve years after ordination I found a wonderful picture that conveyed this image (Exhibit 5).

This image and picture were deeply moving for me; yet, it conveyed a reality that I felt would never be mine. Not because Jesus wouldn't be there and eager to welcome me, but because I was too ashamed to accept his embrace: I was a fraud, not good enough.

Exhibit 5: Home at Last

© 2011 Danny Hahlbohn, *inspired-art.com*. All rights reserved by the artist.

This past November I experienced the desert, another cycle or opportunity for conversion. My mother had not been out of her apartment in over three years. She had reached the point where she would not allow her health aide to care for her and wouldn't take her medication. It became necessary for me to have my mom admitted to a long-term care facility. Though grateful that she had not suffered an accident in her apartment, and that the long-term care facility was professional and loving, I knew I had betrayed my mother. If I had only been more loving, a better son, a truer deacon, I would have been able to care for her myself and make her happy until God called her home. My dream recurred: I was on the toilet, exposed to all for what I am.

Shortly after my mother was institutionalized, I met Brother Donald Bisson and began spiritual direction. He led me to interpret my story, my recurring dream, and the active image in my consciousness of Jesus welcoming the soul into eternity. Through spiritual direction I was able to intellectually understand that the dream was calling me to embrace not only my own shadow, but that of my mother as well. The person on the toilet was the very human person that I was, and that my mother was, and that all God's creatures are: human, loved by God unconditionally, and needing to be loved by me unconditionally. I understood this in my head, but not in my heart; there I was still not good enough.

Ten days before Christmas my mother acted out at the institution. The social worker called to tell me that she would need to be moved onto another unit. I went to be with her before she was moved; she was angry and I was unable, or unwilling, to stay with her during the move. I left the room – the little boy that wasn't good enough to save his dad, the teenager and adult who couldn't fix his mom.

The next evening I experienced a synchronistic event: unexplained, uncontrolled internal bleeding; vast amounts of bright red blood pouring from my rectum. It was a synchronicity on the outside of what I was experiencing on the inside: I couldn't control, couldn't fix my mother, I couldn't stop the bleeding, I was letting go. The next morning I went to the emergency room. The heavy bleeding continued throughout the day and I was admitted to the hospital in the evening. Scheduled for a colonoscopy the next morning, I was required to drink one and one half gallons of a purgative. The directions were to drink eight ounces every fifteen minutes until it was all finished. As I drank this unpleasant cocktail, I looked out of the ninth floor hospital window and was able to see my office window down the street. A bright orange salt-lamp on my desk, that calms my days and that I always keep lit, was visible in the darkness. I fixated on the calming of the lamp as I drank.

In my mind's eye the bright orange lamp became my soul, my authentic Self. I saw the image of Jesus embracing my soul. A staff nurse entered my room and told me that the doctor had asked her to check how much blood I was still losing. I was directed not to flush the toilet and to call her the next time that I went to the bathroom. I followed these instructions. She went into the bathroom as I was standing there watching; it was my recurring dream in waking time. She looked into the toilet and saw the blood. She left and I continued to drink, watching the orange lamp half a block away. And I started to grasp a reality in my heart: I can't fix or rescue anyone; each person is on his or her own journey. I can only love and accept as is, my shadow, my mother's shadow, the shadow of each person with whom I am privileged to journey. And Brother Donald's words during spiritual direction about my recurring dream came to mind: conversion for a good person does not necessarily call them to be better, or do more, but to accept their own and another's humanness, to "take a crap and not feel ashamed." This insight entered my consciousness, and I was aware of the Holy Spirit prompting me to embrace my own human self, my mother's human self; to let God embrace me in my humanness, and to allow God to act through me to embrace my mother.

Spiritual direction with Brother Donald and my own understanding of Jungian insights began to open a window in my psyche. Grace flowed. Energy was released through archetypal activation caused by the active mental image of Jesus in the picture, the orange lamp, the dream, the synchronistic and unexplained bleeding, and the toilet. My unconscious was intervening; the Holy Spirit was pushing and entering my conscious awareness. I slept peacefully. The next morning there was no further bleeding. The colonoscopy found no cause for the bleeding and the doctor had no explanation. I was blessed in being led to recognize the prompting of the Holy Spirit; a prompting to transcend alienation, anger, pain; a call to move towards integration of my shadow, and integration with my mother's shadow; to love her broken human personality; to love my own brokenness, unconditionally. It was one cycle in a lifelong chain, past and future, of conversion opportunities on my journey toward God, my homecoming. Through this insight I came to consciously recognize my authentic Self, in the face smiling at Michael on his promotion day; to consciously recognize my Self, in all its shadowed brokenness, being welcomed home by Jesus; and to recognize the Christ in me embracing my mother's authentic Self, the Christ in her, free of her suffering.

Works Cited

Aziz, Robert. *C. G Jung's Psychology of Religion and Synchronicity.* Albany: State U of New York P, 1990.

Bair, Deidre. *Jung: A Biography.* Boston: Little, 2003.

Belitz, Charlene and Meg Lundstrom. *The Power of Flow: Practical Ways to Transform Your Life with Meaningful Coincidence.* New York: Three Rivers P. 1998.

Bisson, Donald. "Spiritual Direction and Jungian Analytical Psychology." Diss. Pacific School of Religion, 1990.

Bolen, Jean Shinoda, MD. *The Tao of Psychology: Synchronicity and the Self.* 1st paperback ed. New York: Harper, 1982.

Clayton, Philip. "In Whom We Have Our Being: Philosophical Resources for the Doctrine of the Spirit." *Advents of the Spirit: An Introduction to the Current Study of Pneumatology.* Eds. Bradford E. Hinze and D. Lyle Dabney. Milwaukee: Marquette, 2001.

Congar, Yves. *I Believe in the Holy Spirit.* Trans. David Smith. Complete Three Volume ed. New York: Crossroad Herder, 1997.

Costello, John J. "C.G. Jung and Abbe Huvelin." 20 Oct. 2005. <http://www.gaps.co.uk/Papers/Jung_and_Huvelin/.html/>.

Cousineau, Phil. *Soul Moments: Marvelous Stories of Synchronicity – Meaningful Coincidences from a Seemingly Random World.* Berkeley: Conari P, 1997.

Dreyer, Elizabeth A. "An Advent of the Spirit: Medieval Mystics and Saints." *Advents of the Spirit: An Introduction to the Current Study of Pneumatology.* Eds. Bradford E. Hinze and D. Lyle Dabney. Milwaukee: Marquette, 2001.

Hall, Calvin S. and Vernon J. Nordby. *A Primer of Jungian Psychology*. New York: Mentor, 1973.

Hall, Jerome M. *We Have the Mind of Christ: The Holy Spirit and Liturgical Memory in the Thought of Edward J. Kilmartin*. Collegeville: Liturgical P, 2001.

Hart, Russell M. *Crossing the Border: An Introduction to the Practice of Christian Mysticism*. Springfield: Templegate, 1993.

Hilberath, Bernd Jochen. "Identity Through Self-Transcendence: The Holy Spirit and the Fellowship of Free Persons." *Advents of the Spirit: An Introduction to the Current Study of Pneumatology*. Eds. Bradford E. Hinze and D. Lyle Dabney. Milwaukee: Marquette, 2001.

Hinze, Bradford E. and D. Lyle Dabney. "Introduction." *Advents of the Spirit: An Introduction to the Current Study of Pneumatology*. Eds. Bradford E. Hinze and D. Lyle Dabney. Milwaukee: Marquette, 2001.

Jaoudi, Maria, Ph.D. *Christian Mysticism East and West: What the Masters Teach Us*. Mahwah: Paulist P, 1998.

Jerusalem Bible. Alexander Jones, gen. ed. New York: Doubleday, 1968.

Jung, C. G. *Memories, Dreams, and Reflections*. Ed. Aniella Jaffe. Trans. Richard and Clara Winston. New York: Vintage, 1965.

_____. *The Portable Jung*. Ed. Joseph Campbell. Trans. R. F. C. Hull. New York: Viking, 1971.

‗‗‗‗‗‗. "A Psychological Approach to the Trinity." *The Collected Works of C. G. Jung, Psychology and Religion: West and East.* Vol. 11. 2nd ed. Eds. Sir Herbert Read, Michael Fordham, Gerard Adler and William McGuire. Trans. R. F. C. Hull. Princeton: Princeton University Press, 1969.

‗‗‗‗‗‗. *Synchronicity: An Acausal Connecting Principle.* Trans. R. F. C. Hull. 1st paperback ed. Princeton: Bollingen, 1973.

Lammers, Ann Conrad. *In God's Shadow: The Collaboration of Victor White and C. G. Jung.* Mahwah: Paulist, 1994.

McBrien, Richard P. *The Harper Collins Encyclopedia of Catholicism.* Ed. Richard P. McBrien. New York: Harper Collins, 1995.

McDonnell, Kilian, O.S.B. *The Other Hand of God: The Holy Spirit as the Universal Touch and Goal.* Collegeville: Liturgical P, 2003.

McMichaels, Susan W. *Journey out of the Garden: St. Francis of Assisi and the Process of Individuation.* Mahwah: Paulist P, 1997.

Moltmann, Jürgen. *The Source of Life: The Holy Spirit and the Theology of Life.* Trans. Margaret Kohl. Minneapolis: Fortress P, 1997.

‗‗‗‗‗‗. *The Spirit of Life: A Universal Affirmation.* Trans. 1st Fortress Press paperback ed. Margaret Kohl. Minneapolis: Fortress P, 2001.

Montague, George T., S.M. "The Fire in the Word: The Holy Spirit in Scripture." *Advents of the Spirit: An Introduction to the Current Study of Pneumatology.* Eds. Bradford E. Hinze and D. Lyle Dabney. Milwaukee: Marquette, 2001.

O'Murchu, Diarmuid. *Quantum Theology: Spiritual Implications of the New Physics.* New York: Crossroad P, 1997.

Papineau, Andre. Email to author. 5 February 2006.

Peck, M. Scott, MD. *The Road Less Traveled*. 25th anniversary ed. New York: Simon, 2003.

Pratt, John P. "Synchronicity as a Sign." *Meridian* 12 May 2004. <http://www.johnpratt.com/>.

Progoff, Ira. *The Cloud of Unknowing*. New York: Dell, 1957.

_____. *Jung, Synchronicity, and Human Destiny: Noncausal Dimensions of Human Experience*. New York: Dell P, 1973.

Rahner, Karl. *Foundations of Christian Faith: An Introduction to the Idea of Christianity*. Trans. William V. Dych. New York: Crossroad, 1978.

_____. *The Great Church Year: The Best of Karl Rahner's Homilies, Sermons, and Meditations*. Ed. Albert Raffelt. Trans. Harvey D. Egan, S.J. English translation ed. New York: Crossroad, 1993.

Rollins, Wayne G. *Jung and the Bible*. Atlanta: John Knox P, 1983.

Rushnell, Squire. *When God Winks: How the Power of Coincidence Guides Your Life*. New York: Atria, 2001.

Schemel, George J., S.J. "The Place of the Unconscious in Spiritual Direction." 21 Oct. 2005. <http://www.isecp.org/chapt_4.html/>.

Underhill, Evelyn. *Mysticism: The Nature and Development of Spiritual Consciousness*. Twelfth ed. Oxford: Oneworld Publications, 1999.

Vatican II. "Dogmatic Constitution on Divine Revelation." 18 Nov. 1965. *Vatican Council II: The Conciliar and Post Conciliar Documents*. Ed. Austin Flannery. Northport: Costello, 1986. 101–8.

Von Franz, Marie-Louise. *On Divination and Synchronicity*. Toronto: Inner City B, 1980.

White, Victor, O.P. *God and the Unconscious*. London: Harvill Press, 1952.

Made in United States
North Haven, CT
07 October 2024

58390229R00057